Celebrating Intellectual Curiosity

Celebrating Intellectual Curiosity

Kindergarten through College Scholarship and Research

Michael Gose

ROWMAN & LITTLEFIELD
Lanham • Boulder • New York • London

Published by Rowman & Littlefield
A wholly owned subsidiary of The Rowman & Littlefield Publishing Group, Inc.
4501 Forbes Boulevard, Suite 200, Lanham, Maryland 20706
www.rowman.com

Unit A, Whitacre Mews, 26-34 Stannary Street, London SE11 4AB

Copyright © 2017 by Michael Gose

All rights reserved. No part of this book may be reproduced in any form or by any electronic or mechanical means, including information storage and retrieval systems, without written permission from the publisher, except by a reviewer who may quote passages in a review.

British Library Cataloguing in Publication Information Available

Library of Congress Cataloging-in-Publication Data

Library of Congress Cataloging-in-Publication Data Available

978-1-4758-3538-0 (cloth : alk. paper)
978-1-4758-3539-7 (pbk. : alk. paper)
978-1-4758-3540-3 (electronic)

∞ ™ The paper used in this publication meets the minimum requirements of American National Standard for Information Sciences Permanence of Paper for Printed Library Materials, ANSI/NISO Z39.48-1992.

Printed in the United States of America

I dedicate this book to Janice, Creedance, Chris, Sia, and Nolan.

Contents

Foreword ... ix
Preface: Celebrating Intellectual Curiosity ... xiii
Acknowledgements ... xix
Introduction ... xxi

1. The Importance and Context of All Scholarship and Research and a Microcosm of the Macrocosm ... 1
2. The Scholarship of Teaching ... 7
3. The Scholarship of Teaching— Action Research ... 13
4. Creative Art ... 31
5. Arts-Based Research ... 43
6. The Scholarship of Service ... 51
7. Curriculum Development, Administration, Community, Colleagueship ... 61
8. Scholarship of the Student ... 69
9. The Legacy and Ecology of Education ... 79
10. Establishing the Rationale and Grading Policies for Student Scholarship and Research ... 87
11. No Good Deed Goes Unpunished; Virtue Is Its Own Reward: Warnings and Encouragement ... 93

Conclusion ... 103
Appendix A: The New Carnegie Unit ... 113

Bibliography	125
About the Author	127

Foreword

One of my favorite memories from being in Dr. Gose's class is how he used to chide students to refine their analysis of a passage with the Rev. Jesse Jackson line, "a text without context is a pretext" so as I write this I can't help but wonder if a foreword without with an afterword is a word problem. I guess I'll find out.

The first time I met Dr. Gose (simply Gose to many of us), I was a nervous college freshmen, applying to spend my sophomore year studying overseas in the London program, of which Gose was the faculty sponsor.

I had never met Gose, so I wasn't entirely sure what to expect from the interview. I immediately sensed that the process would be demanding because when I walked into his office he looked like what I had always imagined a college professor to look like when I left the farm in Idaho to enroll at Pepperdine. He sported a neatly trimmed beard, and wore both a tartan cap and a tweed jacket. I felt as if I were already in the U.K.

I remained undaunted though because I was prepped and ready to begin my interview. He sat across from me holding the rating sheet, which he was supposed to fill out after asking me a series of questions, but instead of asking me questions he handed me the sheet and asked me to fill it out. I wasn't quite clear what was happening, but I knew that my final evaluation would be favorable because I was the one completing it.

He watched carefully as I evaluated myself on traits ranging from academic ability to self-confidence. When I finished the evaluation he asked follow-up questions about my ratings and what ensued was a rich conversation. In my naiveté I felt that this interview was not as demanding as I had assumed it would be, but like so many interactions with Gose I didn't "get it" until much later in life. I did not fully understand what had taken place in that interview until I began hiring people for the school that I founded.

Like many applicants, I met all of the basic requirements and in a traditional interview I would have likely said things very similar to what other candidates would say. By using a self-evaluation strategy Gose not only created a process for a deeper conversation, but he also was able to assess how I responded to the unexpected and ambiguous, which is a key to success in a study abroad program.

This interview was my first taste of how Gose fostered curiosity in his students. He would create provocative experiences and rarely tell you why. In fact, he never told me why he conducted my interview the way he did, but it was such a rich, unanticipated event that I was left trying to make meaning of it years after it occurred.

Soon after the year in London I enrolled in Gose's curriculum and methods class, where I began to question so much of what is taken for granted in education. I know it's strange but in some ways it seems inevitable that 25 years after completing Gose's class, I've not only started a high school, but as I was reading the manuscript of this book I jotted down ideas for a teacher training program I had begun planning. Gose taught me to pursue my own questions and, as he predicted, it led to me being much more proactive in my life.

This is the kind of full circle moment that we all have in our lives after an experience with a great scholar. We end up engaged in activities that we can easily connect to the time we spent under his/her mentorship. I walked away from studying under Gose, with what you will have after reading this book, an understanding of the complexities of scholarship, and a gnawing desire make sense of it. This is not the kind of desire that comes as a sharp hunger pang, calling you to immediate action, but instead it's a desire that will sustain a pursuit for years. You will finish this book with more questions than you had before you read it. This book will not define curiosity, but instead ignite it, and push you toward a course of action.

Of course, this book is not only about building curiosity. Most importantly this book reminds us of the commitment that we have to one other as scholars. Even though we hear a lot about how technology will change education forever, Gose reminds us that education is done by, with, and through people. We all have a role to play in pursuing scholarship, and it's important to acknowledge that we impact one another in both subtle and direct ways. In fact one of the true gifts of this book is that it is impossible for educators to read it without wanting to unravel their educational DNA and trace the lineage of their practice to the scholars under which they have studied.

It is with that in mind that I wanted to include a few heuristics I gained from Gose which I have shared with other educators:

You take professors, not classes.

In teaching you just take it one day at time, but you signed up to finish the year

Your first year teaching will go really well until they find out that you are nice, then it's all over.

Some times when a lesson is bombing you have to just go out singing.

The best grade is an A- because it means you nailed the content but didn't follow the form.

While it's best not to have a vice, if you do have one, such as smoking cigars, then only smoke expensive cigars. That way you can't afford to do it very often.

You will have to pretend to be angry with a student for the good of the group, even when you aren't. Because you really can't get angry with someone who is five minutes late because he was watching the ducks.

When Ted Williams goes up to bat, you know what he says, "I'm the best f***ing hitter on the planet." When you write something, you need to say that "I'm the best f***ing writer on the planet, and you need to hear what I'm about to say."

Most people only have three really great teachers in their life, your goal is to be one of those three.

As we all contemplate the scholars we've studied under as we read this book, I think that Gose would want you to remember something that the late Eliot Eisner shared with me in his class on educational criticism.

"You can tell a teacher they've done a good job, and it doesn't cost a damn thing."

Gose, you've done a good job.

—Ken Montgomery, PhD, co-founder and executive director of Design Tech High School (d.tech), located on the Oracle campus, making it the first public high school located at a corporate headquarters; d.tech has been influenced and inspired by the ideas of the K12 lab at Stanford's Hasso Plattner Institute of Design (d.school)

Preface

Celebrating Intellectual Curiosity

One of my teachers, Elliot Eisner, wrote about one of his teachers, Benjamin Bloom, that Bloom "embraced the idea that education as a process was an effort to realize human potential. . . . Education was an exercise in optimism" (Eisner 2000, 2). I intend for this book to continue that tradition and legacy of optimism.

This personal connection among scholars also suggests one of the most important themes of this book. Young scholars study with more experienced scholars. Bloom taught Eisner who taught me. Knowledge and the quest for knowledge are handed down in school, person to person.

A researcher looks back. Eisner looked back at Bloom. I have looked back at Eisner and Bloom. In writing this book, I have used numerous ideas taught by Eisner. I have also included a case study as a microcosm of the macrocosm. In 2015, a kindergarten teacher looked back at Bloom's 1956 *A Taxonomy of Educational Objectives* for curriculum development. When enough scholars recognize the importance of new work, it becomes a part of the professional literature. That, too, is part of our legacy.

As the kindergarten teacher's students, they are beginning scholars. As young scholars they were asked to look back, to do research. They were expected to work at higher levels of cognition as they experienced a field trip. They then looked back at their experience to identify patterns. They inherit from Bloom via their own teacher.

This is how it always is, just more obvious in the direct relation of Bloom and the kindergarten teacher. The inter-relationship of scholarship and research K–PhD crosses all levels of schooling and stages of development across generations.

Each scholar inherits from previous scholars. Each scholar learns previously established knowledge and skills. Each scholar K–PhD learns to use those skills, look back at previous knowledge, and develop new understanding.

Simultaneously to my clarifying issues of scholarship and research I want it to be clear that I am celebrating intellectual curiosity. Such is a fragile human capacity. The contemporary near obsession with assessment, standards, and state exams is having unintended consequences. It is dampening curiosity and the quest for new insight and knowledge. Pursuing scholarship and research K–PhD is a hero's journey. (Administrators, logical positivists, and bureaucrats are not necessarily the enemies along that journey, but sometimes it does feel that way.)

K–PhD students need to learn the skills associated with reading, writing, computing, listening, speaking. Instruction can help with the learning of those skills. But K–PhD students also need their curiosity kindled, not extinguished. They need to research their own questions for further understanding.

Eddie Mateer and I both studied in high school under John M. Daly. I eventually went into academia; Eddie went into banking. But we both still think of ourselves as Daly's students. However that affects us individually, we are both scholars in the sense that we studied with a teacher. In ways difficult to describe, our outlooks were shaped by that mentoring teacher.

In a school setting, each student has a teacher, who had had a teacher. Scholarship is not only something studied and written about. Scholarship is the legacy of all the ways teaching-learning, and much more, gets passed down, generation to generation.

Research skills become increasingly sophisticated over the years. Benjamin Bloom produced research results that Laurie Patsalides found helpful to her own work in kindergarten. For formal research to have influence, it must find its way to where it is most needed. Patsalides had to be a scholar and researcher to be able to recognize the prospects of using Bloom's work.

Patsalides was already at work in the first days of her kindergarten class, exerting her role as teacher. Her students became scholars of her teaching. She helped them to solve new problems by looking back at their experiences and looking for patterns in that experience. The process increases human understanding in her own particular corner of education.

Children enter school curious. Good scholarship and research skills start being developed at least by kindergarten. Students and teachers at every level have respective opportunities and responsibilities. The need to encourage curiosity and initiative, scholarship and research, are critical concerns K–PhD. The work advances education by increasing the understanding within students, teachers, classes, schools.

Painter and professor Joe Piasantin observed that he appreciated students who enrolled in his classes who had something to communicate. He preferred them to students who primarily came to learn techniques. Exactly.

Schools have uncountable amounts of content and skills for students to learn. Teachers certainly need to be capable at instruction. But the far greater challenge for teachers is to nurture students so that they follow their own curiosity, ask their own questions, find what they have to communicate, discover what they have best to contribute. Philosopher Jose Ortega Y Gassett (1980, 236) says:

> The solution . . . does not consist of decreeing that one not study, but of a deep reform of that human activity called studying and, hence, of the student's being. In order to achieve this, one must turn teaching completely around and say that primarily and fundamentally teaching is only the teaching of a need for the science and not the teaching of the science itself, whose need the student does not feel.

One trains a seal, educates a person. Students are more likely to be proactive in their own lives if they learn to pursue their own questions. Teaching a skill set outside of a common humanity would be benign at best, and dangerous at worst.

Developing students and teachers as scholars and researchers insures a future of productive and contributory citizens. They will use these skills inside or outside the Ecology of Schools. All students who studied with a teacher are by definition scholars. The most fortunate scholars are those who studied with a teacher who mentored them, who encouraged their curiosity, helped them find what skills, talents, and interests they possessed and could develop to greatest effect.

The best researchers are those who studied with teachers, from kindergarten until having left school, who taught them in as many ways as possible to look back. Students research what they had previously learned and experienced toward puzzling out keener insight into something they questioned, repeating the process, asking better and better questions.

What has actually been going on behind the closed doors of America's classrooms? In his essay *Encouraging Student Research*, educator Douglas Selwyn concludes on the basis of his wide personal experience in visiting classrooms: "Students are not given the time or room to follow their questions to *research* [emphasis added] their interests" (Selwyn 2011, 277).

Teachers may change their behavior when researchers visit their classes. It does not really matter whether the climate for assessment and standards and state exams has constricted teaching-learning, or not. The attitudes and skills for scholarship and research continue to need to be inculcated K–PhD.

Students must mine their own imaginations and experiences to know a subject more completely. Students and teachers need time and space to be scholars and researchers. All educators would do well to remember and retain and preserve the enthusiasm that comes with curiosity, not relegate the privilege only to the hallowed halls of Research I schools.

The sciences have for the most part done a fine job of scholarship and research K–PhD. Students are introduced to the scientific method and conduct experiments. The humanities have used (overused?) the term paper to teach students skills of library research. Students can be introduced at an early age to finding primary sources to establish a history. This book esteems those approaches, but it is not about those well-covered subjects.

Instrumental to any potential for this book to encourage scholarship and research K–PhD is in any clarification it provides about the great variety in meaningful approaches. Secondarily, but of potential help, the book looks at a short list of different criteria that might apply to evaluate different kinds of research. Such criteria can be used to explain and justify important undertakings that do not fit under the more narrow, dominant, limited methods of assessment.

I am greatly indebted to the scholars who have given me the best ideas to work with over my career. But those very best ideas exist because they have been nurtured in an ecological system that depends upon others. Editors and peer reviewers having realized the special qualities of such ideas and gotten them into print and to the attention of other scholars. Other teachers and professors have found those ideas and taught them in class. They used them in writing their own books, articles, and textbooks for all levels of school.

Teachers with informed ideas serve on committees, mentor students, learn new teaching techniques, develop curriculum, prepare assessment reports. The best of the ideas seem to call for lives of service. All of it is important and interdependent. Curious minds pursue and contribute to human understanding.

My own professor and mentor, Elliot Eisner, encouraged all of his students to look for what was neglected or missing. My emphases in this book are six-fold. Why this book? I was:

1. Concerned that assessment has tended to focus only on instruction. Important content and skills are central and essential to any curriculum. The purpose for teaching this legacy of previously acquired content and skills is to encourage students' curiosity and to help them discover how they can best fit in and contribute to the world.
2. Alarmed that the overemphasis on assessment, standards, and state testing has had the unanticipated consequence of damaging that fragile student capacity for curiosity, and of the opinion that we are standardizing instead of setting high standards.

3. Discouraged by how valuing one kind of scholarship can unnecessarily result in a lack of appreciation for other forms of scholarship. Can we all just get along?
4. Encouraged that a wider array of scholarship and research has emerged. These forms deserve greater appreciation and acceptance. They also deserve at least occasional use by all teachers and students to promote full understanding.
5. Heartened by the work of educators who persevere in the face of adversity. While "no good deed goes unpunished," "virtue is its own reward."
6. Hopeful that this book will contribute to human understanding by clarifying some issues of scholarship and research. One does not dilute the highest standards of scholarship and research by encouraging all students and teachers K–PhD to involve themselves in pursuing questions in school.

The intention of this book is to clarify, encourage, and appreciate the many manifestations of scholarship and research K–PhD. It is all part of an ecology that increases human understanding. Thinking and feeling. Teaching and learning. Practice and policy. Art and science. Generally and specifically. Normally and unusually. Depth and breadth. Teachers and students. Using what we know best, while taking calculated risks to get better.

Acknowledgements

Having been a student for twenty-eight years, and having been a teacher for forty-nine years, I have far too many teachers, fellow students, and students to thank here. (I will mention, however, that I finally had my second-generation student. Former student Robert Escudero and his wife Julie recently saw their son, Bobby, enroll in one of my courses.)

When telling my school story, I focus on what I remember as the most important individuals to me. I emphasize the importance of teacher John M. Daly, the aid and comfort of fellow student Eddie Mateer, and my delight in one of my own students, Charlie Park. This book allows me to tell the fuller story, one that realizes that every teacher, fellow student, and perhaps one's own students, make schooling both possible and meaningful.

I am particularly indebted to Jennifer and Eric Wolford. They created the Michael Gose Scholarship that led to the formation of a group that met weekly. Jeff Pippin, Heidi Jaeger, Sally Bryant, Brita Lundberg, Dylan Shapiro, and Madison Blin were among the most regular participants. We spent a year exploring creative art as an act of scholarship and research. Those meetings were instrumental to the creation of this book.

While I alone am responsible for the content and quality of the book, I am indebted to the wisdom of Publisher and Vice President, Tom Koerner, who encouraged me to broaden the scope of my original manuscript, and who had me focus on intellectual curiosity. I was well supported by the team at Rowman & Littlefield: Carlie Wall, Associate Editor, Emily Tuttle, Assistant Editor, and Caitlin Bean, Production Editor.

I had countless conversations with colleagues about issues of scholarship and research. Joi Carr, Paul Begin, David Holmes, Stella Erbes, James Thomas, Sonia Sorrell, Craig Detweiler, Robert Escudero, Tomas Martinez, Genny Moore, Ken Montgomery, Gretchen Batcheller, Ty Pownall, Ben

Postlethwaite, Lee Kats, Joe Piasantin, Don Shores, Christopher Parkening, Dino Nicardos, Sarah Attar, Jordan Hess, and Alexis Allison were particularly helpful.

I was most fortunate to have studied with Stanford University Professor Elliot Eisner. I think of the Alexander Pope line, "oft thought, but ne'er so well expressed." This book relies very heavily on ideas and language developed by Elliot to account for the importance of complementary forms of scholarship and research. I do not apologize for being biased; it is at least arguable that Elliot Eisner was the most important writer in education of the past fifty years. His voice has been missed following his death at age eighty in 2014.

Am I now getting to an age where I can appreciate even the resistance to otherwise good ideas that might improve education? No. Absolutely not. I will, however, acknowledge that conflict makes for better stories, and that I am profoundly indebted to schools where I have spent all but my first four years of life.

Introduction

> Curiosity is one of the permanent and certain characteristics of a vigorous mind.
> —Samuel Johnson

> The first and simplest emotion which we discover in the human mind, is curiosity.
> —Edmund Burke

Celebrating Intellectual Curiosity: Kindergarten through College Scholarship and Research seeks to call attention to the big picture that unites all academic endeavor into a critical and generative whole.

This book offers four major themes for the reader's consideration.

First, intellectual curiosity drives understanding. As a fragile characteristic, it needs to be protected and nurtured K–PhD.

Second, the skills associated with teaching-learning, scholarship-research, service, and colleagueship need to be developed in *all* students K–PhD.

Third, not only do all forms of research need to be appreciated, utilizing them more widely will make for a healthier ecology of education.

Fourth, with all due respect for the superstar scholars and researchers, the ecology of education requires a diversity of educators and students attending to their own scholarship and research responsibilities to increase human understanding.

What is intellectual curiosity? This book uses *intellectual curiosity* and *curiosity* interchangeably. Curiosity is certainly not limited to school; in fact, all too often it may be limited by school. The intellect, the mind, combines thought and emotion. Because schools are better recognized for working with the intellect, the term "intellectual curiosity" locates curiosity in an educational setting. That is not particularly fair, for example, to autodidacts, but nonetheless, the term remains primarily associated with schooling. As a term, "curiosity" suggests inquisitiveness, the need to ask questions, to investigate, to explore, to find answers. An appreciative sense of scholarship and research provides the skills to pursue one's questions more effectively.

This study seeks to enhance scholarship and research by calling attention to the importance of recognizing the fullness of what they entail for all students and teachers K–PhD. Academic specialization, the scholarship of discovery, and depth are incredibly important. However, they are not the subjects of this book. This book emphasizes what have been the more neglected forms of scholarship and research. A wider sense of scholarship and research must also be a vital part of all education. This book is about appreciating curiosity and all the tools of scholarship and research that can be utilized K–PhD.

This work emphasizes exploring what it means to be a scholar from an early age (study under a master) and a researcher (to look back), whether artistically or systematically. This work celebrates the intellectual curiosity that leads to exploring questions to find answers. Relatively few young scholars will ever end up writing an article accepted by a refereed journal, but all students need to develop their curiosity and their research skills.

Students also need to develop the other skills expected of those scholars who publish in refereed journals. Students and their teachers have obligations beyond teaching-learning. They also need to develop skills for research, service, and colleagueship. Each of these areas requires careful nurturing K–PhD. All research formats contribute. Cutting-edge research advances knowledge. Students and teachers as scholars and researchers advance human understanding.

What is there to know about the many, varied forms of scholarship/research?

1. They are important.
2. Most tend to be underappreciated.
3. Each form has its own set of complications.
4. One set of criteria are not adequate to assess all forms of research. Finding appropriate criteria for evaluation will make it easier to understand what was undertaken, and whether it was successful. Finding appropriate criteria for various forms of scholarship and research will also help establish a professional rationale for decision makers who control policy and funding.

Most chapters offer vignettes for points 1–3, and then a potential set of criteria that may be appropriate and helpful for evaluation of the respective form of scholarship.

With the perceived emphasis on specialization, teachers are reluctant to use the gamut of research forms that could contribute to the overall success of all students in the classroom. Students and teachers benefit by being scholars and researchers in multiple ways.

For example, John Dewey posited that knowledge is not complete until the student has an emotional connection to it. Understandably, a history teacher might be most comfortable testing a student in chronology. But allowing students to experiment with creative artistry, for example, to make a film about history, would solidify knowledge of that subject. Alternatively, the art student might do well to read in history before undertaking a painting inspired by Picasso's *Guernica*. Teachers of all subjects would do well to balance their own curricula. Scientific and artistic considerations need to inform one another.

What would such diversity in approaches require? Having appropriate ways to grade student work would remove a major obstacle. Confidence in grading would make it more possible and likely for teachers to work outside their usual comfort zones.

One of the challenges is to find appropriate criteria for evaluating such variety in student work, a topic for chapter 10. Two separate considerations from that chapter are worth bringing up now so that the teachers reading this book will realize that this is a very feasible idea. First, all assignments do not need to be graded in the same way. When inviting students to experiment with a form of research outside one's usual area of expertise, the teacher can evaluate the *educational significance* of the work. Did the painting for the history class capture something about what was learned? All teachers have the expertise to evaluate the educational significance of student work.

Students' service and artistic work can also be evaluated by the standards of arts-based research discussed in chapter 5. These criteria also provide teachers an apt way of evaluating work that is less conspicuously related to the specific academic content of a course.

A good practice here is to use criterion referenced rather than norm referenced standards. A set amount of points could be given instead of a letter grade. The points would be given if the assignment was done *well enough* not to have to be done over. Such a practice could be used on occasion K–PhD.

The second major consideration here is whether the student results are to be measured by science-based or art-based criteria. The fallback position in education continues to be dominated by scientific-like expectations. *Action research*, for example, usually calls for a *systematic* gathering of data. From a more normative, qualitative, and artistic perspective, the artist is the instrument. The artist takes in an experience of what is being studied, and then, more intuitively than not, expresses a response in an appropriate medium. There are established criteria for evaluating the success of artistic endeavors.

This is covered in chapters 4 and 5. A teacher does not have to be an artist, per se, to use these criteria to evaluate student work.

Like kindergarten teacher Laurie Patsalides, teachers K–PhD benefit from having studied the work of elite scholars. Her own students benefitted from studying with her. All benefit from engaging in the pursuit of questions, and from looking back (research) at previous experience and learning.

Exploration can be discursive (proceeding by reason) or nondiscursive (more dependent upon intuition). Most exploration is most probably some of both. Most likely, scientists follow questions that they have an emotional attachment to. Artists ordinarily appreciate when someone can articulate in a discursive way something that they have achieved artistically.

Elite researchers must have the highest, most rigorous standards for results that have implications for the whole. All students and teachers K–PhD contribute to human understanding by understanding their particular situations.

The emphasis here is on encouraging the willingness to entertain diversity—appreciate differences; diversify scholarship and research. Enhanced attention to the lessons of scholarship and research in their broadest terms K–PhD assuredly increases human understanding in each nook and cranny of the school experience.

Most teachers (and professors) engage in scholarship and research. The professors at research universities gain the most recognition for their discoveries of new knowledge. But the entire educational system relies upon all of its members, administrators, teachers, students, and their constituencies to grapple with what is unknown to increase human understanding.

The brightest mind may make a discovery, but other minds have to comprehend the new idea, evaluate its significance, and disseminate it accordingly. As in the case in chapter 1, the kindergarten teacher worked effectively with the ideas of Benjamin Bloom, a professor of education at the University of Chicago and editor of *A Taxonomy of Educational Objectives* (1956).

Unfortunately, only one-third of Bloom's original paradigm became persistent in education. Bloom identified three domains of knowledge—the cognitive, affective, and psychomotor. Bloom hoped for a holistic approach in schooling that united all three domains. Regrettably, only his cognitive domain has been widely utilized.

The thought here is that if the teachers and administrators had been as wise as Bloom in their own scholarship and research, the ecology of the educational system would be even healthier. The suffusion of the best ideas throughout education relies upon its participants to use responsibly their own skills of scholarship and research.

This book anticipates the charge that it dilutes what higher education has specialized in—a highly constricted view of scholarship and research. The argument here is that education needs to reclaim the original meanings of *scholarship* and *research* because they are terms common to educated people.

Originally, a scholar studied with a master. At every level, schoolchildren study with someone who has mastered skills that they seek to obtain. Research originates from the French word *réchercher* and simply means "to look back." The kindergartners struggling to apply the rules they have previously learned, the artist looking back and choosing from techniques previously developed, the doctoral students doing thorough reviews of the professional literature, are all researchers. They all grow in understanding. Curiosity starts at birth and deserves to be sustained in schools.

Stanford professor and historian David Tyack once mentioned in class that he thought that the quality of teaching was inversely related to the number of years the class of students had been in school. He thought that the experience gap between a kindergartner and the teacher was the largest gap and thus required the most accomplished teaching.

K–PhD teachers have varying degrees of academic skills, but on the whole the hypothesis here is that every level of schooling demands every kind of scholarship and research. All parts inform the whole.

Having previously studied from their own teachers, each educator has some degree of discernment. From K through the PhD, students and teachers scrutinize new ideas that enhance their own understanding. They then look back at what they have been doing and determine if they might do something even better. Education requires all of its constituencies to be scholars and researchers for a healthy ecology of the whole.

How is the book organized?

Chapter 1 emphasizes the importance of all scholarship and research. It uses a case study of the report of a curricular innovation by a kindergarten teacher. In this example, a work of scholarship from 1956 continues to inform practice in 2015. The teacher's report evidences the ecology of education at its healthiest.

Chapter 2 looks at the scholarship of teaching and the acts of scholarship/research that intend to inform a large professional audience about its implications and results.

Chapter 3 examines the scholarship of teaching as action research. The audience for this research may be as small as the individual teacher or an individual student. It also looks at how the criteria for evaluating this kind of research may be very different than the criteria for more formal research.

Chapters 4 and 5 make a distinction between creative artistry and arts-based research. Both are seen as vital acts of scholarship and research. However, creative artistry is more likely to be evaluated on the basis of aesthetic criteria, whereas arts-based research emphasizes the educational significance of the results (and that the artistry need only be good enough to communicate intended findings).

Chapter 6 discusses the importance of a scholarship of service. All school-related service activities are inherently informed by previous school experience. They cause participants to look back on their previous knowledge and experience toward completing a service activity. Service can involve informing; creating a vehicle for others to use in an educational way; and/or a full-service, volunteer effort. The thought here is that the participants somehow often learn more than they contribute. They also have opportunity to master the long-term social skills that are inculcated in the total school experience.

Chapter 7 emphasizes the importance of curriculum development as an act of scholarship and research. It also looks at administration and colleagueship in terms of scholarship and research.

Chapter 8 argues for the importance of recognizing a scholarship of the student. Students have a vital role to play in scholarship and research that is related to, but different from, what is expected of their teachers.

Chapter 9 integrates all the above considerations on research and scholarship into how it all works together in a biofeedback and generative fashion. The chapter discusses the ecology of education. The thesis is that K=1, that Knowledge is One.

Chapter 10 continues the theme of big-picture thinking by considering how scholarship and research pertain to the social skills learned in school and the long-term effects of the school experience. The chapter also includes recommendations for how teachers can justify and develop a rationale for devoting time to approaches to scholarship and research that they have not used before.

Chapter 11 offers both warnings and encouragement for students and teachers to go beyond the common place to expand efforts at increasing human understanding.

This book concludes with thoughts on developing students as scholars and researchers, setting high standards instead of standardizing, reemphasizing how art and science work together in an integrated educational ecology, a defense of teachers, and final observations.

The appendix offers a proposal for a New Carnegie Unit that would help compare different forms of scholarship and professional expectation on a more equitable basis among college professors. The New Carnegie Unit adds a professor's investment-of-time standard as a part of the evaluation of scholarly research activity. It also suggests a method for comparing and weighing research and scholarly activities.

A MAJOR CAVEAT ABOUT SPECIALIZATION, DEPTH, AND THE SCHOLARSHIP OF DISCOVERY: NOTABLE SCHOLARS AND CUTTING-EDGE RESEARCH

At least by middle school, teachers specialize in specific subjects. Professors almost always have advanced degrees. Expertise may require highly specialized knowledge in a very narrow specialty of a single academic discipline, or in having expansive knowledge across areas that pertain to a specific problem or issue. For example, one might have a specialty in chemistry, or alternatively be a gastrointestinal specialist.

"Depth" is the watchword for advanced degrees. Professors have been educated to create new knowledge in their respective degree areas. Colleges and universities legitimately expect each and every professor to create new knowledge and present the results for professional review. Such activity validates the professor and contributes to a growing knowledge base.

Depth is fundamental to scholarship and research. The author celebrates and depends upon notable scholars doing cutting-edge research. That work is honored.

However, the search for increased understanding also requires breadth. All students and teachers have vital roles as scholars and researchers. Breadth, curiosity, and that all teachers and students are scholars and researchers are emphases in this book.

> It is a miracle that curiosity survives formal education. —Albert Einstein

A cautionary tale. The first year, precocious college student was enrolled in the Honors Introduction to Chemistry class for majors. The students had weekly labs. One particular week the students did not get their expected results. But they wrote up the results that they did get and turned them in, done for the week.

With the exception of this one student. He wanted to know why they had not gotten the expected results. Over the next six days he set up a new set of experiments. By the next class he had an answer. To his great dismay at that next class session, neither the professor nor the other students were interested in what he had found. That was last week, this was this week.

This student dropped the major at the end of the semester.

Without fail, scholars must cultivate the curiosity of their budding scholars. The work of the chagrined student was the ultimate reason to learn to do research—generate a question and find an answer. Curiosity propels the pursuit of knowledge. Curiosity must be tended carefully.

This book celebrates curiosity and the rich possibilities of scholarship and research K–PhD.

A note: With permission some of the stories use real names. Other stories use fictional names and the details have been altered to protect the usual suspects. The core meanings of the respective stories remain intact.

Chapter One

The Importance and Context of All Scholarship and Research and a Microcosm of the Macrocosm

> The disposition to continue to learn throughout life is perhaps one of the most important contributions that schools can make to an individual's development.
> —Elliot Eisner

> The important thing is not to stop questioning. Curiosity has its own reason for existing.
> —Albert Einstein

THE IMPORTANCE OF THE BROADER UNDERSTANDING OF SCHOLARSHIP AND RESEARCH

Seemingly small details of scholarship can have lasting effects. High-school teacher John M. Daly decided on his own accord that the high school history text that was provided to him by the school district was inadequate for preparing his public school students for college. Thus, he assigned Harvard professor and author T. A. Bailey's *The American Pageant*. His students really had no choice but to buy the book on their own.

Requiring public school students to purchase a textbook was a clear violation of any number of rules and laws. But Daly was never sanctioned by any school administrator. He reflected upon his own Princeton college experience. He considered the potential of his students, and what he thought they needed. He remembered his own experience as a scholar and what would be an appropriate textbook for college-bound high school students. He came to a decision. His students would be better prepared for Harvard if they read a college-level text written by a Harvard professor.

For his college-bound students, that was an important decision in readying them for admission at selective schools. His choice was an important one, and his decision was based on his own scholarship and research. It is a good example of the ramifications of scholarship and research in the ecology of education. Presumably millions of important decisions are made by teachers that are clearly based on an overall understanding of scholarship and research.

Scholarship is equal, only some scholarship is more equal than others. Not every high school student would profit from a college-level text. But Daly's did. The more scholarly textbook had to be matched by a scholar to his more scholarly students.

THE POLITICS OF SCHOLARSHIP AND RESEARCH

If the one example above suggests the importance of scholarship and research, a second example will hopefully remind the reader that matters of scholarship and research have their own set of complications

At a selective Christian college, two proposals competed for one summer grant. The first sought to do an oral history of the only known Japanese-speaking church in that denomination. The group not only had cultural significance for this Christian college, it was a group that would go on to contribute $500,000 to the school's scholarship fund. The other grant proposal sought to measure the changing temperature of robin eggs in local nests over that summertime.

Is there any doubt whatsoever that even in the context of a Christian college that the presumed rigor associated with the science proposal would be seen as far more important? It was assuredly the science proposal that was funded. While logical positivism has contributed mightily to the college's understanding of rigor, its dominance in higher education continues.

The scientific study was perhaps more obviously scholarship of discovery. That form of scholarship has been valued (and well-funded). But scientific scholarship has too often been funded at the expense of other forms of scholarship. What about the educational and cultural significance of research proposals?

The point here is that different forms of research have their own claims to importance. More than one criteria might well apply to deciding which ideas will be best supported by money, time, space. All forms of scholarship and research contribute to the whole.

THE MICROCOSM OF THE MACROCOSM

The example of kindergarten teacher Laurie Patsalides and her online article on the Bright Hub Education website suggest the ecology of scholarship and research at its finest.

Patsalides explained her task: "In the school where I taught, we were presented with a challenge to review the levels, choose a topic, and plan lessons to teach Bloom's taxonomy across all of its levels. (Patsalides 2015). She reported that she eventually chose to use the taxonomy in conjunction with a field trip. She summarized her challenges in trying to have her kindergartners work with each level of Bloom's taxonomy. The taxonomy's assumption about cognition is that students can move from remembering to understanding to applying to analyzing to evaluating to creating. Patsalides reported that one of the rewards was the challenge to push students to the higher levels of cognition. N. L. Gage explains that was a purpose of the taxonomy. "The greatest value of the taxonomy and related documents has been its influence . . . (on) more kinds of cognitive activities . . . many teachers . . . do not often venture higher in the taxonomy" (Gage 1979, 54–55).

Celebrating Intellectual Curiosity posits that this is a great example of how the ecology of education works at its best. In 1956, Benjamin Bloom edited *Taxonomy of Educational Objectives*. In 2015, Patsalides wrote an account of using a 2001 revision of that taxonomy to create a lesson for her kindergarten students. The taxonomy named after the editor, Benjamin Bloom, was actually the work of many.

The development of the taxonomy included the *American Psychological Association*, a large group of college and secondary school teachers, administrators, curriculum directors, and educational research specialists (Bloom 1956). The taxonomy was influential, and it was eventually modified in 2001 by Lorin Anderson and David Krathwohl. One of the most obvious changes was at the top of the taxonomy. In the 1956 version, Synthesis was the fifth stage and Evaluation the sixth. In the 2001 revision, Evaluation had fallen to fifth and Synthesis had been upgraded and reenvisioned as Creativity.

Bloom had indicated in the 1956 edition that the work was tentative and should be subject to revision. He added that, "a final criterion is that the taxonomy must be accepted and used by the workers in the field if it is to be regarded as a useful and effective tool. Whether or not it meets this criterion can be determined only after a sufficient amount of time has elapsed" (Bloom 1956, 24).

The taxonomy has been in use for seven decades. It has been identified as one of the very most influential works in American education. Time has determined that the taxonomy has indeed been useful and effective. For sixty years it has informed practice, and practice has informed theory to the extent that the original theory was modified. That is how it works in the ecology of scholarship and research. Each part informs the whole and although teachers are involved with different combinations of theory and practice, all teachers are scholars and researchers.

The ecology of scholarship and research K–PhD enlarges human understanding. Appreciating and utilizing the myriad of forms of scholarship and research can help teachers K–PhD improve the vitality of teaching and learning.

For the teacher, the most basic form of research is often called *action research*. Richard Sagor defines it as "a disciplined process of inquiry conducted by and for those taking the action. The primary reason for engaging in action research is to assist the 'actor' in improving and/or refining his or her action" (Sagor 2000, 1).

This describes Patsalides's *Putting Bloom's Taxonomy into Practice*. She wrote, "In the school where I taught we were presented with a challenge to review the levels, choose a topic, and plan a lesson to teach Bloom's taxonomy across all of its levels" (Patsalides 2015).

Sagor (2000) identifies seven steps that are typically involved in action research: (1) selecting a focus, (2) clarifying theories, (3) identifying research questions, (4) collecting data, (5) analyzing data, (6) reporting results, and (7) taking informed action.

While it is often thought that action research is teacher initiated, Patsalides indicated that hers resulted from a challenge from an administrator. She reported that she spent several weeks working on the task. She studied Bloom's taxonomy. She considered the developmental levels of her kindergartners. She arrived at the choice of a field trip for her lesson. She paralleled the field trip with a reading selection. This indicates that she was conscientiously and systematically making and remaking her plans. And in this case, she both reported her results as well as the fact that this lesson motivated her to do similar lessons thereafter.

Furthermore, even though her students were only in kindergarten, Patsalides introduced them to a very similar set of behaviors. Her students engaged in their own equivalency to action research. Her students were asked to focus on some aspect of their field trip. They were introduced to the stages in Bloom's taxonomy through the kinds of questions they were asked. They were asked to compare their field trip experience to what they read in a nonfiction book. The teacher wrote down their observations. The students were then asked to think about what the other students had written. Eventually the lesson led to students creating pamphlets. Students were engaged. As Sagor describes, action research "is a disciplined process of inquiry conducted by and for those taking the action. The primary reason for engaging in action research is to assist the 'actor' in improving and/or refining his or her actions" (Sagor 2000, 5). Both the teachers and the students were engaged in activity that can be described as action research. While it does not replace other forms of teaching and learning, the overriding point here is that scholarship and research inform all educational decisions. Recognizing and encouraging all forms of scholarship strengthens the whole.

Gary Anderson and Kathryn Herr (1994, 29–32) suggest five criteria for practitioner research: democratic validity, outcome validity, process validity, catalytic validity, and dialogic validity. Patsalides seemingly met those criteria quite successfully. She worked in collaboration with all involved, which included administrators, other teachers, and the students themselves. Her description of the field trip used to implement Bloom's taxonomy met the expectation to create such a lesson. She reported an involved and complex process of determining what to do. Her enthusiasm was clear. She reported her dialogue with students about their experience.

A heuristic time was had by all. Teachers K–PhD can learn from her example.

The tendency to focus only on what one is good at limits a complete education. While it is understandable that teachers will focus on what they do best, finding time to experiment with all the forms of scholarship and research can enhance teaching and learning. Patsalides went beyond her comfort level. She tried something new. She reported that this led her to try other things, like having her students create a pamphlet at the end of the school year for the next year's students.

There is no competition among lighthouses. At its best, the system takes what it needs from the best sources. Human understanding is increased when kindergarten teachers like Patsalides work with the best ideas from the best researchers and encourage students to seek out answers. The system works better when at least someone in higher education works to insure that the best ideas are disseminated clearly throughout the system.

A healthy ecology of scholarship and research depends upon K–12 schools not being too isolated from higher education and vice versa. The professors making those connections with textbook writing, teacher preparation programs, and K–12 schools perform exceptional academic service central to scholarship and research having legs.

Other lessons suggest themselves from this case. This example of extremely influential scholarship crossed numerous lines of demarcation. Bloom was only one of the scholars involved in the original piece that was the *Taxonomy of Educational Objectives*. The work was also an integrative piece across the fields of psychology and education. Bloom intended for the work to be useful, and Patsalides is but one example of a scholarship of application. That the work made it more possible for a kindergarten teacher to coax higher cognition from her students is surely a scholarship of service.

Patsalides's work was also an example of the scholarship of curriculum development. Her students' work at creating pamphlets shows the early traces of creative artistry and/or arts-based research. Involving students in reaching their own conclusions is the foundation of the scholarship of the student.

Her work and the report of that work was commendable. Any evaluation demands to be overwhelmingly positive. Dewey indicates that the purpose of criticism is the reeducation of perception. Any criticism here must necessarily be positive, constructive, and gentle. Bloom's intent was to help teachers push their students toward higher levels of cognition. Patsalides did that.

The case also points, however, at why research in higher education insists upon expert review. All of the above suggests that the students' learning was overwhelmingly positive. The editor did a good job of reporting change in how Bloom's taxonomy had been revised. However, the reported results have overinterpreted the higher levels on the taxonomy—for example, whether on the original or the revised list, evaluation requires more sophisticated cognitive skills than one could expect from a single lesson.

Patsalides actually anticipates this concern as she writes about how difficult evaluation was for her students given their developmental levels. And in a sense here is the rub as we the collective try to increase human understanding throughout schooling. Patsalides's work benefited from working with the ideas associated with Bloom's taxonomy. And Bloom himself recognized the difficulties in language, some overlap in terms, but that the taxonomy could be helpful to communication. It has been overwhelmingly so. But even it remains subject to misunderstanding and the need for clarifications where and when needed.

At its best, scholarship and research permeate the ecology of schooling K–PhD and to change metaphors, with checks and balances throughout the system.

Chapter Two

The Scholarship of Teaching

> I'd rather learn from one bird how to sing than teach 10,000 stars how not to dance.
>
> —e. e. cummings

Ordinarily professors are more likely than K–12 teachers to have the time and opportunity to write authoritative books in their respective fields. Yet retired high-school teacher Monty Steadman wrote the comprehensive and authoritative book *Coaches' Guide to Cross Country and Track and Field: Training Cycles* (2014). Thoughtful, literate, curious, with fifty or so years of coaching, Steadman by example makes the case for the importance of practitioner knowledge brought meaningfully to a public audience.

THE SCHOLARSHIP OF TEACHING IS NOT ONLY ABOUT FINDINGS

The literature on action research finds great value in the collaboration of teachers with those who perhaps have more advanced expertise in matters of research. Advanced Placement and Honors English had much greater credibility among high-school students because English teacher Alice Coleman had worked with a professor from San Diego State University to bring Advanced Placement to Mission Bay High School. Furthermore, it was reported that she was working on a book with that professor. Scholarship and research has many faces. Sometimes the role model of someone engaged in scholarship and research has more importance than any published results by the scholar-researcher.

Mrs. Smith—referred to behind her back by both critics and fans as "Granny Smith"—took it upon herself to prepare to teach her students the

New Math. (It is difficult in hindsight to establish which particular *New Math* this one happened to be.) The new *New Math* textbooks looked more like workbooks than textbooks. They were described as a draft, a work in progress.

Many of Smith's students went on to collegiate success in mathematics. Smith went above and beyond with her scholarship of teaching. Her students at least eventually appreciated that commitment. Mathematicians and math educators wanted better-prepared students entering college. They had to work with the math, the textbooks, the districts, the schools, and the teachers. The curriculum progresses when the scholarship of teaching engages the entire educational system.

Scholarship of discovery is for naught without the scholarship of teaching.

THE SCHOLARSHIP OF TEACHING AND NORMATIVE ISSUES

The scholarship of teaching is not without its complications.

The social science professor rather detested true/false exams. True or false: Christopher Columbus discovered America in 1492? Well, can one discover something others had already found, whether by the people living there or even discovered earlier by another European explorer, perhaps Leif Erikson? And since Columbus didn't reach the continent, does it still count as discovering America? True or false?

Frito-Lay had a contest on whether it was true or false that the Dodgers moved to Los Angeles in 1958. Well, the front office moved in 1957, and the players moved in 1958. So are the Dodgers the organization, or the team? Whether something is true or false can be complicated.

Nonetheless, true/false questions remain in play with teachers, so the social science professor determined to do a meta-analysis of all the research on the topic.

Somewhat to the professor's chagrin, there was indisputable proof that effective true/false questions can be written, even ones that test higher orders of thinking. Such questions also offer the advantage of testing more subject areas in a similar amount of test-taking time.

Fine.

Except that there was also pretty much definitive proof that teachers never take the time to write true/false questions that are actually excellent. Most of the true/false questions actually written by teachers are almost entirely at the lowest level of knowledge, the rote. Furthermore, there is evidence that students may remember what they read, thus remembering a false question as actually being true.

From a strictly scientific point of view, meaningful true/false questions can be written. But from a more normative point of view, the one more associated with meaning, is it worth it to promote true/false questions knowing they will most likely be trivial? Scientifically, the research establishes the potential efficacy of true/false test items. How, then, is one to regard the evidence that good true/false items are, however, almost never written? How are the qualitative and normative issues of research and scholarship to be adjudicated?

Research can inform but not answer the value questions.

UNDERAPPRECIATED SCHOLARSHIP

The professor was pulling an industrial-size dolly stacked high with six-inch-thick accreditation reports for some mass assessment audience. Having been involved in such activities, the author had a keen appreciation that even the writing of a book does not take the time and effort pulling together an accreditation report takes. Also, writing a book is much less frustrating. If such official reports are required, the teachers must be involved. Perhaps the time spent is partially service, but it must necessarily involve major acts of research (looking back).

The person literally pulling the load was getting absolutely no credit for this required effort of scholarship. She received no compensatory time to undertake other scholarship that year. Faculty participants might be a bit less beleaguered if their work was recognized and appreciated for all that it is—scholarship of teaching by the pound, carted by a dolly.

VALIDITY AND THE SCHOLARSHIP OF TEACHING

One of the most famous studies in education was a massive study of how teachers use classroom time. The study was by an imminent scholar, but one who might have benefitted from more time working in a public school. This scholar studied how schoolteachers use classroom time. Probably out of kindness of heart, he notified each teacher whom he was studying when he planned to observe. Hmmm. How valid is the research?

A school administrator was responsible for evaluating classroom teachers. During one of his classroom visits, he noticed that some of the students were trying to stifle snickers. He had decent rapport with students on campus. He could not resist the temptation to ask a student what was up? He was told that the teacher he was observing had never before given a lecture to this class.

Of course! Presumably most teachers suspect that outside observers expect a teacher to have great control over a class. The usual thought is that a lecture is the easiest way to control a class (which over the weeks of a term is probably not actually true). Because this teacher had been notified of the visit, the teacher performed as presumably expected. She did this even though she had never previously lectured to this class.

This administrator realized that it would be preferable in the future to indicate to teachers that a visit was likely due in the next week or so, but to drop in otherwise unannounced. The result was that he usually found better teaching going on than when that same teacher had time to prepare for what s/he thought was expected by an administrator.

The famous researcher's team, unfortunately, always gave plenty of advance notice of a pending visit. Thus this educator suspects that all the very ambitious study's findings were largely skewed in reporting that teachers spend most of their time in front of the class. A scholarship of teaching needs to be nuanced in ways perhaps difficult for outsiders to appreciate.

CLASSIC ISSUES IN THE SCHOLARSHIP OF TEACHING

The teacher left his undergraduate program thinking that James Joyce's *Ulysses* was the greatest literary novel. The next year as a tenth grade high school English teacher, he and his class discovered S. E. Hinton's novel *The Outsiders*. He remembered the adolescent joy of reading a great story. For some of his students it was the first book that they had ever read in entirety.

Reading tasks are developmental. Great reads like *The Outsiders* contribute to human understanding. The pleasure may lead some students eventually to the challenges of Joyce.

English Literature Professor James Thomas wrote a book on *Harry Potter*. Was Harry worthy attention for a distinguished literature professor? Be assured that the question was asked, eyebrows raised. The answer has to be, "Of course!" The Rowling series drew Thomas's attention. The voluminous hours he spent on researching and writing on the subject were obviously personally meaningful. As a senior faculty member, his effort was not necessarily about advancement of the field, but about growth, and enjoyment, and personal fulfillment.

The book and his subsequent college class have been very meaningful to his school and the students who eagerly enrolled in the class. His book has been purchased by other professors, and also by K–12 teachers. History will decide if *Harry Potter* will be widely considered *Literature* at the collegiate level. Studies like that of Thomas's will help decide whether Rowling's work makes the cut.

Having a larger school audience consider the Potter series more seriously, and discuss it more deeply, can only contribute to greater understanding.

Rowling's work has had a powerful, worldwide influence, regardless of its final assessed merits as a work of art.

Quite possibly Thomas will have advanced his field by having expanded its purview rather than having found a rival to James Joyce. Again, there is no competition among lighthouses.

Certainly, established scholars like Thomas have earned the freedom to explore their keenest interests. That is also where the greatest advancement of human understanding will likely take place—from well-pursued questions that curious scholars/researchers care about.

The value of the Potter research is a normative issue that cannot be settled by any amount of research. It takes time to evaluate what the culture will determine to be classic.

THE POLITICS OF THE SCHOLARSHIP OF TEACHING

As written in the introduction, the head of the Dean's Honors Program wrote a tongue-in-cheek, first person article about a nature trip taken with students and sent it to a prestigious ecological journal. He heard back rather immediately that "we don't print that kind of article here." About six weeks later he received a letter from that same journal. "We've changed our minds. We'd like to publish your article." They made it the lead article of a subsequent issue. The editor explained, "Ordinarily we do not publish this kind of article, but there is something here important to consider . . ."

As a biofeedback system, scholars need to pay attention to signals that may come from unexpected sources, from voices tending to go unheard.

What is biofeedback? "Biofeedback is the process of gaining greater awareness of many physiological functions primarily using instruments that provide information on the activity of those same systems, with a goal of being able to manipulate them at will. Some of the processes that can be controlled include brainwaves, muscle tone, skin conductance, heart rate and pain perception" (Wikipedia).

"Biofeedback may be used to improve health, performance, and the physiological changes that often occur in conjunction with changes to thoughts, emotions, and behavior. Eventually, these changes may be maintained without the use of extra equipment, even though no equipment is necessarily required to practice biofeedback" (Wikipedia). The editor wrote the professor that it had been a difficult choice, but the ecological journal integrated the biofeedback that it had otherwise been disposed to ignore. This is seen here as a good thing.

CRITERIA FOR THE SCHOLARSHIP OF TEACHING

Different schools, different courses, different groups of students often invite creative problem solving. Creating a different teaching strategy, an innovative assignment, a creative new curriculum, or a handbook that students actually want to read all require important scholarship. But the evidence of success within this scholarship differs greatly from the standards of scholarship in the subject matter.

Probable criteria include: did the innovation *work*; did it help students learn? Did it engage students more deeply? Did it reveal some of the imagination and creativity behind the work produced as part of the traditional scholarship within the field? Was it original, imaginative, creative? Sometimes, when extremely well done, the innovation may be picked up by another professor, another program, another school. But this is not necessary for appreciation of this kind of scholarship.

The utilitarian standard is the greatest good for the greatest number. Developing interesting course materials that become a textbook used by other schools would be a particularly noteworthy accomplishment. Much good would be done for many people. But the development of a handbook that helps students who previously struggled with a subject now master that subject evidences significant benefit, if only for the limited number of students of that teacher.

What, then, is the scholarship of teaching? Ernest Boyer's definition (1990) includes expertise in the subject matter, knowledge of methods, and commitment to growth. That short list tends to penalize some faculty members more than others. For example, what about some faculty members who are asked to teach outside of their fields to cover a pressing need?

Some scholars will continue to produce meaningful scholarship on teaching, and do so for common consumption and publication. The emphasis of this book, however, is that all teachers need to engage in an action-research version of the scholarship of teaching (see the next chapter). And for the most part, that work does not require the time and effort that goes into publication. That kind of scholarship of teaching realizes that specific needs in specific places may very well require solutions that do not necessarily generalize.

Chapter Three

The Scholarship of Teaching — Action Research

> It is teachers who in the end will change the world of the school by understanding it.
> —Lawrence Stenhouse

> The whole art of teaching is only the art of awakening the natural curiosity of young minds for the purpose of satisfying it afterwards.
> —Anatole France

Juan stuttered badly. He had tried for years to gain help from the district speech therapist but had never been seen. The teacher tried to help. He read everything he could find about stuttering and even bought a small tape recorder to try one of the techniques. But to no avail. All his research was for naught. His student still stuttered.

So the teacher redoubled his efforts by stalking the district's much beleaguered speech therapist until the expert saw Juan. By the end of the year Juan no longer stuttered. That's how the ecology of scholarship and research works. Eventually human understanding was increased. The teacher's action research failed. But he managed to connect the student to the source of knowledge that was required. The success represents a healthy ecology of scholarship and research. In this case the emphasis was on action.

THE NEED FOR ACTION RESEARCH IN TEACHING

The history professor was from Harvard. In Jean Anyon's (1980) terms about social class and the curriculum, he presented himself as one of the social elite. His emphasis was on original, individual works and discussion. The class would not be required to read any textbook. That would be untoward. Too middle class to have someone else synthesize an academic field for future scholars. Except in fact what was expected on his exams was what a student could only find in a traditional textbook on that class's subject matter. Students appreciated the assigned, nontextbooks, but on exams those same books only made sense in terms of what was traditionally taught about history in the unassigned history textbooks.

It is not so much that the teacher was a hypocrite. He was unaware of what kind of teacher he was. His own action research into his own teaching might have helped him recognize the disparity between his teaching and his testing. Lack of action research in this case results in poor practice despite his substantial Ivy League knowledge of history.

The hidden costs of specialization include the consequent tendency to conclude that one should only do what one is good at. Somewhat ironically, there are times when one might become better at one's specialty by delving into other areas outside one's comfort level. This can be especially true for the scholarship of teaching.

The story on the Framework College campus was that former Little All American football player Donald Armstrong did not readily transition well to the job of assistant coach. Apparently in his first practice with the incoming first-year offensive linemen, he repeatedly showed the players how to execute the forearm rip by putting a succession of student-athletes on their rear ends. Yet despite his very excellent demonstration of technique, he was reported to have been baffled that none of his students were subsequently able to demonstrate that skill. Perhaps the difference was that Donald was known to be able to bench press 450 pounds?

The usual presumption in sports is that the most natural athletes are not usually the best teachers. Those who had to do the most learning to survive on the playing field often know the most learnable skills. The study of all the skills necessary to success is an important, critical aspect of scholarship and especially for making knowledge accessible to students.

In terms of the scholarship of teaching, Armstrong knew how to teach a technique that students were incapable of duplicating. Action research connects the teaching to the particular students.

Enough is known about developmental psychology and developmental reading to do better than making all tenth grade students read George Elliot's *Silas Marner*. An academic case can be made for George Elliot and for *Silas Marner*. But what about the adolescent students who learn to hate the subject of English literature because they hate *Silas Marner* so much. The point here is that eventually no amount of subject matter scholarship can inform the qualitative choices that a teacher must make. Perhaps action research about educating students would have permitted that teacher to have given some lifeline to the students who hit the brick wall of *Silas Marner*.

ACTION RESEARCH EMPHASIZES THE PARTICULAR

For the teacher, N=1. That is, what will work for a specific teacher will be a combination of skills, talents, interests, and predispositions that will be different from other teachers. This truism severely impacts any scholarship of teaching. While those in an area like teacher education might want to study how teachers in general use classroom time, the individual teacher in most academic areas will be much more concerned about what techniques might improve his or her own individual performance with particular groups of students.

The fourth period literature class had gone swimmingly. The exact same lesson was bombing dreadfully with sixth period. With more than a little exasperation the teacher cried out, "Fourth period loved this lesson."

A brave student raised his hand.

The miffed teacher acknowledged that hand.

"Mr. Hermanson, we aren't fourth period."

In a millisecond, the student had been more effective at the early rounds of action research on teaching than the teacher had been. No amount of research on teaching accounts for why a lesson works with one class and not another. Only with action research can a teacher have the prospect of matching a lesson with a specific class.

As another example, a rhetoric professor in an undergraduate liberal arts college was not having the degree of success that he wanted. He received very good student evaluations, but this was not enough for him. Given the argument here that there are only so many hours available for the scholar, he could have maintained the status quo and continued to spend all his remaining available time on his research agenda.

However, he elected to spend time researching teaching (looking again, and again at his own teaching, as well as looking to colleagues, students, books, articles, workshops). He found some personal answers, especially from a respected senior colleague. The hypotheses included that his syllabus was too organized. The research on teaching indicates that when a teacher is too prepared, the teaching will be inauthentic. The teacher will tend to force the lesson rather than respond to the class's needs.

This teacher had what other research terms *withitness*, but this characteristic went underutilized because of a schedule he himself had set for the syllabus. This professor went to a more topical syllabus, freeing up class meetings for more give and take. The professor also changed from a testing system that emphasized concrete bits of knowledge to a system that emphasized working with more abstract concepts. The next set of student evaluations indicated that the changes had been well received and very successful.

At the university level, why is this research of one's own pedagogy generally only covered under teaching, instead of the *Scholarship of Teaching*?

Another professor at the same school has received good student evaluations for a lengthy career . . . and is known not to have changed lecture notes during all of that time. That teacher puts in the same number of classroom hours, and a similar amount of time grading a challenging amount of student assignments. In terms of hours on the job, both spend a similar amount of time on teaching, per se.

However, given the limited number of additional hours available for scholarship, a fair reward system need recognize the above and beyond work that the rhetoric professor brought to important research on the scholarship of teaching. All subsequent classes of students benefitted from the changes the professor made, changes based in inquiry, research, scholarship, and the professional literature on teaching.

But weren't the improved student evaluations ample evidence of the worth of the effort? And even if it hadn't worked, wouldn't the effort have been worth the time? This professor had made meaningful personal changes, but *not* in ways that demanded that further time be spent to write it all up, whether as a prospective journal article that would not be published, or even for a Rank, Tenure, and Promotion committee. The benefits to the teacher and his students were more than ample.

Such important action research scholarship and research warrants credit and recognition K–PhD.

A LACK OF ACTION IN ACTION RESEARCH

The graduate student in religion was studying Christian churches' responses to racism. S/he found a clear, cogent, timely article with very smart ideas about solutions. Belatedly s/he noticed that the article was several decades old. An inherent problem of research implications is their dubious relationship to the possibility and likelihood of actual change.

MATH OR MATH EDUCATION?

The Math Department at Strong College, Popular University includes those with PhD degrees in mathematics, but also at least one professor with a degree in math education. While the historical debate has been on whether the teachers of K–12 students are best prepared by work in the subject matter, or work in education, in fact math professors who teach are preoccupied with education, and math educators who teach are preoccupied with math. The necessary balance between the subject matter and the teaching-learning concerns come down to individual needs and choices and preferences.

This duality suggests the appropriateness of evaluating college professors on both their scholarship in their subject, but also on their scholarship in teaching their subject. Presumably, individual careers would evidence quite different balances between the two concerns. While an individual teacher might do a better job with one than the other, both are quite necessary in the context of teaching and even college teaching. Both need evaluation and appreciation.

The latitude on evaluating scholarship in subject versus scholarship in teaching, however, is quite different. The scholarship in the subject matter will most often utilize the methods and lines of inquiry most recognized by colleagues in that field. While different subjects, for example math versus art, may have quite different standards, with perhaps the exception of cutting-edge innovations, the peer-review system or editorial review generally work reasonably well.

The same is not true for the necessary work in the scholarship of teaching. Different schools, different courses, different groups of students often invite creative problem solving. Matching the subject matter with specific groups of students poses a significant educational challenge. Creating a different teaching strategy, an innovative assignment, a creative new curriculum, a handbook that students actually want to read, all require important scholarship. However, the evidence of success within this scholarship differs greatly from the standards of scholarship in the subject matter.

WHEN RESEARCH DOES NOT INFORM PRACTICE

Schooled in higher education that emphasized more elite and rarefied forms of research, the beginning teacher did not think of what he was doing as action research. Nor did he recognize that his results in studying teaching and developing curriculum were more dependent upon artistic paradigms. A student approached him with a personal problem for which he had actually taken a college course. He literally had a stack of articles in his desk that contained the best scholarship and research available at the time on that topic.

Absolutely none of it was useful for helping this one student. None of it. And the teacher had no prior experience with the problem. (But fortunately he was able to use his research skills to find a human resource since the printed materials had failed him.)

Scientists and social scientists typically look for generalizations by gathering as much data as possible. Artists tend to do research by looking back at what can be generalized from one example. Perhaps not systematically, but conscientiously the teacher poured over his past experience to find what might, in some way, be sufficiently comparable as to be helpful to what his educational psychology professor had termed *the unencountered exemplar*.

Action research includes the specific teacher and specific students as critical variables.

What might well be included in the scholarship of teaching as action research? As a first response, rather than reinventing the wheel, researching the vast, already existing professional research on teaching suggests time well spent. However, what about those remarkable occasions when the teaching question has not been previously studied?

DANTE—DIFFERENT CONCLUSIONS FOR DIFFERENT TEACHERS?

Hopefully no scholar would agree that there is only one way to teach. Take Dante's *Divine Comedy*. Experience suggests that students connect with its *Inferno* much more than its *Purgatory* or *Paradise*. For reasons Dante well understands, it is a lot more fun to think about who all deserves to be in the respective levels of Hell than of Heaven. How much classroom time is spent in America on *Hell* versus *Purgatory* and *Paradise* could be an empirical question. But do teachers of Dante have any doubt about the answer? Even a Dante fanatic who insists on more time being spent on *Paradise* would do so knowing that such a practice was highly unusual.

Perhaps a better empirical question would be whether students having attended more closely to the *Inferno* are limited in their own understanding of the work by the narrator's early confusion. Dante does not come to true clarity until the end of *Paradise*. The abundance of *definitive texts* is contained in the later cantos of *Paradise*. For understanding the ideas of *The Divine Comedy*, perhaps it would be academically more sound to study and discuss the work backward—starting with the last canto and handling the work in reverse order. Understanding Dante's clarity at the end clears up all the earlier confusions. However, would not such an approach do a disservice to an aesthetic appreciation of, perhaps, the greatest poem of Western culture?

Perhaps the work should be read a first time beginning to end, and then a second time end to beginning? Most teachers probably struggle to get students to read the work in its entirety even once.

Thus how to teach *The Divine Comedy* invites more normative questions than empirical ones. Furthermore, and just as important, the answers to these questions undoubtedly vary teacher to teacher, student to student, class to class. In any given semester, however, the professor necessarily makes decisions about how to teach a timeless work at that particular time and place to those particular students.

A scholarship of teaching assumes value in the teacher spending time not only on a reread of *The Divine Comedy*, reading notes, and lecture notes, but also on the *research* on one's specific group of students. The study of the students is necessary to connect effectively the work and the students to yield meaningful learning.

Knowing ahead of time that researching one's students is at best educated guesswork, what kinds of questions might be considered to help students make contact with the material? Asking such questions elevates instruction to teaching. One's students can find any number of lectures on the Internet about Dante. These canned lectures may or may not have value, but they most definitely have not been tailored to the individual and class needs of a particular course. For a tailored class, the material might be expected to fit more expertly.

For mere instruction, readings are selected, course topics set, work assigned, content delivered. Students meet or do not meet expectations. If all students were already committed to advanced degrees in the subject, perhaps instruction suffices. However, except perhaps at the most advanced graduate-level classes, students do not likely have that level of background and commitment. Thus, those who prefer to teach may well ask a litany of empirical questions about their students.

Whereas the Dante issues focused on *The Divine Comedy* content questions, the students themselves who are studying Dante are worthy of action-research scrutiny. The answers to such questions likely differ teacher to teacher, class to class.

A CASE EXAMPLE OF THE ADVANTAGE OF ACTION-BASED RESEARCH IN TEACHING

A repeated argument in these pages is that a very wide variety in research and scholarship counts and that teachers tend to make valuable use of their discretionary time. According to the teaching load, teachers and professors do not have the same amount of such time in a work week. A teaching staff necessarily needs to be diversified to cover the myriad of needs in a learning community.

A college advisor once misguidedly had all of his Honors students enroll in four courses from four great teachers in the same semester. Overload. Quite possibly even the best students cannot handle the demands of more than one or two great teachers at a given time. Meanwhile, progress in the overall curriculum must continue. Covariably, one of the best published and worst teachers was also valuable, in different ways, to the students and to the university.

One noted professor managed to achieve excellent student evaluations without having changed his/her class notes in decades. Because that is true, s/he had more discretionary time to spend on publications. However, if scholarship is to reside generally in the academy, the work other teachers and professors do in improving their teaching and developing their curriculum needs to be recognized for the research and scholarship that it is. Perhaps the best definition of scholarship is, indeed, the work done by a scholar. Such a definition invariably covers the breadth and width of research and scholarly activity.

This study began by considering artistry, teaching, and curriculum development as activities based in research and scholarship. Belatedly, the potential and value of deliberately *researching* the students in a given class became apparent. Such activity can be very time consuming, and certainly above and beyond the traditional expectations of teaching a subject to a group of students.

The conclusion is that such research into students as students is a frequent, if an above and beyond undertaking, among teachers who teach activity based classes. Those who teach such courses as PE, acting, dance, painting, sculpture, filmmaking, drawing, public speaking, debate, etcetera are especially likely to study their students to help figure out what will allow the individual student to improve.

All teachers need to engage in such research at least to some extent. Experience shows that it can be extremely valuable to the individual student, and a very good use of the forementioned discretionary time. A professor was teaching a speech class in a residential program in London. A highlight of the course was students giving a speech at the legendary Speaker's Corner in Hyde Park. A heuristic time was had by all. The course's speech textbook emphasized that students find the practices that best suited their individual abilities at delivering a public speech.

Especially because it was a small class and in a residential setting where the professor lived within the same facility, and because there were frequent group activities in London, he had unusual opportunity to talk with the students in multiple settings. The students and professor were able to talk about their different speeches from a number of different perspectives. He felt that each student gave at least one excellent speech. He thought that his research and then coaching helped each student to give that best speech. He had extensive opportunity to study students and help them gain perspective on what their strengths and weaknesses might be, and how to play to the strengths and protect against the weaknesses.

He found the process very much like the form for conducting other social science research. (1) He'd identify the problem. For example, a student's speech might have been stilted. (2) Instead of reviewing the *literature*, he spent hours reviewing video recordings of the students' speeches. (3) Instead of describing the instruments and the population, he matched particular ways of delivering a speech with each student in this class. (4) Traditional social science research often involves a specific treatment to be implemented with a test group. The group will usually be based on some sort of random sample. The results are usually understood in terms of normal distribution. Such results are an extremely valuable consequence of that scholarship. But the general results do not necessarily fit individual students. A treatment that works with a population as a whole may not work for outliers.

The argument here is that at least upon occasion the teacher may find it a very valuable use of the allotted time for research and scholarship in studying his/her own students. The professor found that the time spent on curriculum development for a class to be taught in London, and the extensive time spent in researching his particular group of students, was time well spent, and very much acts of research and scholarship. The international program invited such use of professional time. Finding the time and place for teachers to conduct their own action research could in the long run be very cost effective in terms of maximizing student learning.

The concept of Carnegie Units (appendix) helps *justify* this use of time. There are only a certain number of hours in each day. Such activities tend to be severely underappreciated in the academy. The implied judgment is that a professor can voluntarily choose to spend such time, but only after having taught and completed a full quota of publications during that same time period. That suggests the reason that some professors cannot teach their way out of the proverbial paper bag, but are lauded for their more obvious research and scholarship.

The argument here is not that published research is not extremely valuable. However, for the sake of the entire learning community, the university needs a fairer way of recognizing that it expects diversity in the many ways that its professors conduct research and scholarship for the benefit of the whole. Meanwhile, teachers at all levels need and deserve the support and time to do action research on their own classes and teaching.

IN MY MOTHER'S ACADEMY THERE ARE MANY MANSIONS

Probable criteria for evaluating action research as a form of the scholarship of teaching is similar to the criteria for all scholarship of teaching: Did the innovation *work*? Did it help students learn? Did it engage students more deeply? Did it reveal some of the imagination and creativity behind the work produced as part of the traditional scholarship within the field? Was it original, imaginative, creative? Sometimes, when extremely well done, the innovation may be picked up by another professor, another program, another school. But this is not necessary for appreciation of the work of this kind of scholarship.

The utilitarian standard is the greatest good for the greatest number. Developing interesting course materials that become a textbook used by other schools would be a particularly noteworthy accomplishment. Much good for many people. But the development of a handbook that helps students who previously struggled with a subject now master that subject also evidences a very large amount of good, if only for the limited number of students of that teacher.

In subject matter education, professors might profitably experiment with methodologies developed by other disciplines. An art student might profitably be asked to write a history of the development of one of his/her own paintings. A history student might be asked to paint a picture that captures how the student understands, emotionally, a time period. In terms of subject matter education, the teacher has undertaken an empirical work in that s/he has studied experience that led to an innovation.

The effort is research in that the teacher relooked at what had been done, and then sought out a better way of teaching. The art student benefits from writing a history, but is not expected to meet the same degree of rigor expected of the history student. The history student benefits from the heuristic experience of painting to explore the understanding of history through a different mode of representation. This student, however, cannot be expected to meet the aesthetic criteria that would apply to a student majoring in art.

Appreciating the duality between the subject matter and the subject matter education becomes critical for a complete sense of the scholarship necessary for full success as a teacher. The university gains recognition from the award-winning book written by the professor who cannot teach her/his way out of the proverbial paper bag. The students benefit from the teacher who discovers the myriad of ways to insure that teaching becomes learning, although such cannot be at the expense of rigor in the taught field. At the extremes, the nonteacher might be better off at an R and D center; the nonscholar might be better off teaching at a precollege level.

The emphasis is on the necessary diversity in teaching as well as diversity within the individual teacher's career. By virtue of being a teacher-scholar, scholarship/research in both the subject matter and education in the subject matter are vital.

Gary Anderson and Kathryn Herr (1994, 29–32) offer a definition of validity for practitioner research that is more pertinent to most action research on teaching. They argue for five criteria for practitioner research. Their work is summarized by Colleen McLaughlin (2004, 15–16).

1. Democratic validity: the extent to which the research is done in collaboration with all parties who have a stake in the problem under investigation, and multiple perspectives and interests are taken into account.
2. Outcome validity: the extent to which actions occur that lead to a resolution of the problem under study or to the completion of an action research cycle.

3. Process validity: the adequacy of the processes used in the different phases of the research such as data collection, analysis, etcetera. This validity includes the issue of triangulation as a guard against viewing events from one data source or perspective. It also goes beyond research methods to include several general criteria such as the plausibility of the research.
4. Catalytic validity: this validity describes the degree to which the research energizes the participants to know reality so that they can transform it.
5. Dialogic validity: the degree to which the research promotes a reflective dialogue among all the participants in the research.

These were the criteria used to evaluate Patsalides's work.

SOME SUGGESTIVE QUESTIONS AND ISSUES FOR ACTION RESEARCH BY INDIVIDUAL TEACHERS BASED ON THE TEACHER EDUCATION LITERATURE

How many peers/colleagues/faculty members of any traditional academic discipline are likely to have sufficient knowledge of the research on teaching to make reliable and valid summative conclusions about a colleague's teaching? For example, was the evaluated teacher a mimetic or a transformative teacher? Did the teacher appropriately use behavioral objectives, instrumental objectives, or expressive outcomes?

Within the curriculum what is the relation of the cognitive, affective, and psychomotor domains? What model or combination of *models of teaching* was employed? Was the professor teaching from/to a working-class, middle-class, affluent-professional, or social-elite style of teaching?

What Sort of Academic Students Actually Enrolled in This Class?

An introductory class may very well have an advanced student who was required to come back and take this class for graduation. Some students may take the course as a required course for the major, others as a general education requirement, and still others as an elective. Their backgrounds, interests, and sources of motivation will likely be very different. On occasion, a course may be required for two different majors. For example, while economics majors and business majors are ostensibly interested in similar topics, what the students expect in practice from a macro or micro economics course are generally radically different.

While this generalization will not fit every student per the respective business or economics major, the business majors will likely prefer more concrete and practical course content and assignments. The economics majors may be expected to tolerate, and even prefer, more ambiguity and theory.

Having researched the kinds of students one has, a teacher will do well to experiment with a variety of approaches, readings, strategies, and assignments so that all students maximize learning.

What Are the Social Class Implications for This Class of Students?

Again, while all students will not fit the generalizations, students from different social classes tend to have different orientations, expectations, and preferences. Students from working-class backgrounds are more likely to prefer well-delineated workloads with clear reward structures. Middle-class students are also likely to want clear expectations, but to have more autonomy in meeting those expectations. The students from affluent-professional backgrounds will likely resent, for example, multiple-choice exams, but thrive on independent and creative projects where they can express themselves. Students from a social-elite background will expect course readers or original, seminal work, lots of discussion, and essay exams.

The scholarship of teaching will include a consideration of the social class expectations of the school as a whole, whether that tendency also tends to be true for this subject matter, and for this particular group of students. What are the likely social-class conflicts, and how do they influence the delivery of this particular course to this particular group of students? How many assignments? How much variety in the assignments? What testing format? How much homework will students be expected to do? How difficult might the readings be? Such questions are very time consuming and they do not have to be asked by an instructor. However, the teacher who pursues such questions deserves recognition for this scholarship of teaching.

How Will I Motivate These Students?

Related to the social-class considerations discussed above, some students respond to rewards and punishments, others to the guilt squeeze, others to challenges to their pride, and still others come self-motivated and may resent obvious motivational techniques. Any single class will likely be comprised of students who respond very differently to the same motivational strategy.

Optimally, a teacher will create the amount of anxiety that yields the greatest amount of student achievement. The curve is shown in figure 3.1. Too little anxiety yields low achievement, but so does too much anxiety. And no student is the same. Thus the scholarship of teaching requires the individual teacher to monitor studiously where individuals and the class as a whole are with regard to anxiety and achievement.

The scholarship of teaching also recognizes that reward systems need constant alteration. Praise may work one time and not another. Again, the scholarship of teaching requires constant research into how the past influences present decisions about how to best motivate students. Instruction may not require such effort, but teaching does.

What Are the Rhythms of the Term?

The scholarship of teaching demands research into the probable and actual rhythms of the term. Students do not work equally hard equally long on a day-to-day basis. College fraternity and sorority pledging will influence the entire campus and class, as will a major event on campus including a major sporting event, holidays, vacations, midterms, natural disasters. Mondays versus Tuesdays versus Wednesdays versus Thursdays versus Fridays. Early morning and night classes have their own challenges. An hour-long class requires different pacing than a longer class.

Is the study of such mundane teaching issues important? Important enough to warrant consideration as scholarship? The answer must be yes if justice is to prevail in how teachers are evaluated because the answers to such questions often enhance their degree of classroom success. Scholarship of teaching deserves recognition for those teachers who transcend mere instruction.

What should count as a scholarship of teaching is also an epistemological question. What constitutes valid knowledge? What counts as valid scholarship? Reasonably effective instruction can occur without research into one's

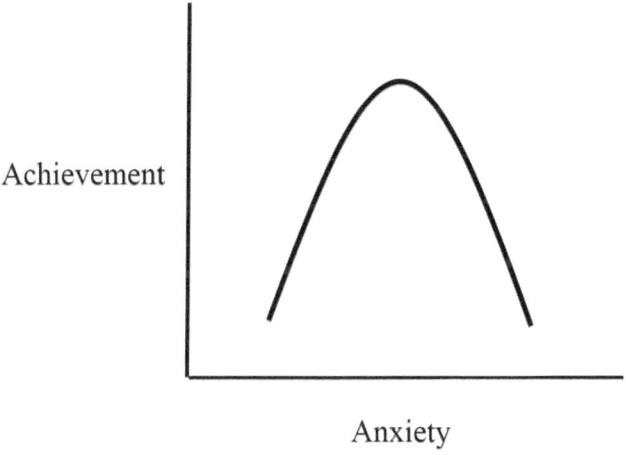

Figure 3.1. Anxiety-Achievement curve

own class of students. A reasonable amount of learning can still occur. The amount of time spent on such scholarship of teaching can otherwise certainly be invested elsewhere. But the respective choices deserve to be weighted fairly in teacher evaluations.

How would one compare the discrete amount of knowledge added to a subject matter through an academic article versus an additional discrete amount of learning added by each student in one's class? First of all, this is not a competition. Both are valuable. Second, the only argument here is not to fail to appreciate the scholarship of teaching. Presumably the assumption must be that in an institution that offers classes to students, very high value is placed not only on covering requisite areas of knowledge, but on as much learning by students as possible. Teaching (vs. instruction) requires research and scholarship about the students and their fit with the course.

What Teaching Strategies Should Be Used, and How Should They Be Organized?

John Dewey argues for the psychological organization of the curriculum. While one's subject matter may (or may not) have agreement about its structure, studying students' responses to the content informs the pacing, variety, strategies that are adapted over the course of a term.

How Will Learning Be Best Evaluated?

Predetermined point systems for grading are highly problematic. How does a teacher know how truly difficult one's assignments will be until studying the student results? Surely every teacher finds some unintended ambiguity in a course assignment or exam? That for whatever reason a particular aspect of the course was a bit misunderstood? That the certain students who did well on a particular exam did so because they had previously had a related course? The scholarship of teaching demands constant vigilance and study of one's own grading practices and the students' responses to the assignments.

If one does use multiple choice or true/false questions, have the results been studied for validity and reliability? Standard error of measurement? Have multiple choice items been scrutinized for difficulty and discrimination? Has the exam been created with regard to a table of specifications, such that what has been tested corresponds to the most important aspects of the curriculum covered?

All assignments need not be graded. Learning for learning's sake is sometimes feasible. All the remaining assignments need not have a letter grade. Criterion referenced evaluation can result in a predetermined number of points for students. A system of + v+ v v- 0 mimics the A, B, C, D, F grading scales but usually with less student angst.

What Needs to Be Added to Keep the Course Fresh?

The scholarship of teaching requires the constant search for some new approach that will keep the course alive and vibrant. If only because a teacher's enthusiasm tends to correlate with student achievement, a course needs to be updated, not only to accommodate new findings in the field, but to avoid becoming boring, predictable, and rote.

WHAT TALENTS AND NEEDS AMONG THE STUDENTS CAN BE INCORPORATED INTO THE CLASS?

Finding the students who can tutor others, those who can speak up for the class, those who are isolated, those who can give accurate feedback to the teacher, those who can contribute to the class process, all deserve the study associated with vital scholarship of teaching.

Is the teacher practicing transformative teaching, or mimetic? Is the teacher teaching to the whole person, or instructing only with regard to a very specific body of knowledge or skill set? Which model or models of teaching does the teacher employ?

Especially at the college level there are questions about class size, lower division or upper division, general education or major. What aspect of teaching? Goals? Teaching activities? Organization of activities? Evaluation? Motivation? The curriculum or the hidden curriculum? The cognitive, affective, and/or psychomotor domain?

What is the context for the professor's scholarship of teaching? Learning theory? Experimentation with methodologies?

To what extent does the scholarship of teaching reflect a knowledge of the research literature on teaching-learning?

Developing a lecture might very well be an act of scholarship of teaching. But Ernest Boyer (1990) recommended that the research on teaching be written up for peer review. Really? Maybe on rare occasion. But the teaching profession mainly needs the kind of scholarship of teaching that helps match what deserves to be taught with the students at hand. Is there teaching without learning? Not to any real extent.

Thus, minimally, the scholarship of teaching might meaningfully apply to such activities that are suggestive of action research:

- Reading to keep up with developments in one's field.
- Reading more widely so that a course's knowledge is set in a larger context.
- Developing teaching-learning activities and studying/reflecting on their seeming success, or lack thereof.
- Studying one's students to better determine what might work best.

- Studying the research on teaching and evaluation.

All of the above are acts of both research and scholarship. All of the above activities can be critical for success with students.

The key result is success with that class's students. All of the results of the above are toward teaching that group of students more effectively. All the scholarship of teaching activities is potentially important.

The results do not need to work for or be adopted by any other teacher or any other students for them to have been important and meaningful.

Thus occasionally, more likely rarely or not at all, the results might be worth spending the time to write up for some other teacher or professor to spend the time reading.

A professor published a classroom innovation in *Learning Magazine*. How would it be evidenced whether magazine subscribers actually tried it? Writing up that innovation was probably worthwhile. But legendary teacher Sylvia Ashton Warner warned against keeping copies of one's lessons, because it is more important to keep the act of teaching fresh. Quite possibly a successful innovation with a particular class will not looked polished, and will be better for not being so. Students respond better to the here and now, and glossy materials turned in by professors to university Rank, Tenure, and Promotion committees should be seen as suspect.

Some additional thoughts on the scholarship of teaching:

It seems terribly inefficient to require a faculty member already well respected for excellence to spend the time that could be used to improve teaching, meet with students, serve on a committee, or continue a research agenda to do the busy work increasingly demanded in the name of assessment.

The superstars usually establish themselves early; those not well suited for professorship usually reveal themselves quite early. Institutions mostly pick teachers who are dedicated and good fits for the particular school. So unless there is a problem, why not spend much less time in evaluations that won't make much difference, and concentrate on helping those teachers and professors who need the most help to do their best work?

The Varied Benefits of Action Research by Teachers

Colleen McLaughlin observes that "there is a growing body of evidence about the effects of practitioners engaging in research and enquiry. First we see that through engaging in research teachers gain a better understanding of their practice and ways to improve it. This often involves close studies of children's learning or curriculum innovations . . . as well as examining theories that are part of educational practice" (McLaughlin 2004, 14–15).

She cites such advantages as:

- Gave teachers an enhanced sense of the student's perspective in the classroom.
- Resulted in a renewed feeling of pride and excitement about teaching.
- Reminded teachers of their intellectual capability.
- Allowed teachers to see that the work they do in school matters.
- Encouraged teachers to develop an expanded sense of what teachers can and ought to do.
- Restored a sense of professionalism.
- Action research on teaching likely has great short-term and long-term benefits for students and teachers.

Chapter Four

Creative Art

Art is humanity's most essential, most universal language. It is not a frill, but a necessary part of communication. The quality of a civilization can be measured through its music, dance, drama, architecture, visual art, and literature. We must give our children knowledge and understanding of civilization's most profound works.
—Dr. Ernest Boyer, Carnegie Foundation for the Advancement of Teaching

Every child is an artist. The problem is how to remain an artist once we grow up.
—Albert Einstein

Scholars K–PhD deserve frequent opportunities to engage in creative art. Precocious work needs to be recognized.

The following is an example of a short story written by a second-grade student. K–PhD students need ample opportunity to explore their own creativity. The author clearly references the "Who Was" series of books. The author clearly transformed those biographies into her own story.

The 5 Lucky Birds
By: Sia Kresch (2nd grade, Mrs. Threlkeld)

It was a nice and sunny day. People were just waking up. But something was wrong. In an apartment there lived a little boy with his mother. Just then, the sun disappeared.

"Mom," said the boy. "What happened to the sun?"

"I don't know," she said.

Suddenly, there was a hole in the sky. It started to grow bigger and bigger. Then it blew wind.

"What's happening!?" screamed the boy.

His mother turned around.

"Oh no!" she said.

Quickly, she ran over to a lever and pulled on it. There was a nice and shiny book.

"This will help us," she said.

The title was *The 5 Lucky Birds*.

"It says here that through the hole will come five people from the past," the mother said.

"What five people?" asked the boy.

"I don't know," said his mother. "But we must get outside."

The boy quickly grabbed his jacket and ran outside. His mom followed him. There was already a big crowd outside. The boy and his mother pushed and shoved their way through. Suddenly, they saw a figure coming down.

It was Walt Disney! He was holding a stuffed Mickey Mouse.

Next came Roald Dahl, who was holding a pencil, clipboard, and paper.

Then came Queen Elizabeth the First. She was wearing her crown.

Out of the hole popped Leonardo da Vinci. He was holding a piece of wood, a screw, and a wrench.

Finally came Amelia Earhart. She was holding a map.

The five people looked around. Walt Disney saw an animation store called "Movie Stars" and quickly ran in. Roald Dahl saw a place to write called "Writers at Work" and zoomed in. Queen Elizabeth saw a jewelry shop called "Shimmer & Shine" and went in like a big blob of jelly. Leonardo da Vinci saw a painting shop called "Color for All" and pretended to walk stairs. Amelia Earhart saw a plane store called "Fly High" and drove in.

Now everyone was busy, leaving everybody left with the rest of the day. That night it was very hard to sleep. There was a lot of banging.

The next day, Walt Disney asked if anyone would like to see the movie he made, called *Snow White and the Seven Dwarfs*. People ran into the movie theater.

Roald Dahl asked if anyone would like to hear his story, called *The BFG*. A bunch of kids raced into the library.

Queen Elizabeth asked if anyone would like free jewelry. Girls ran as fast as they could run.

Leonardo da Vinci asked if they wanted to paint. Families marched in.

Amelia Earhart asked if anyone would like to watch her fly a plane. Families came walking on to the grass.

The boy and his mother went back to their house. The mother read the book.

"It says that when it's a full moon they will all go back," she said. "That's in two days, exactly!"

Again, it was very hard to sleep that night. The next morning, Walt Disney asked if anyone would like to see how to make a movie. "Yeah!" they said.

Roald Dahl asked if anyone would like to write a story. Grown-ups followed him.

Queen Elizabeth asked if anyone would like to put on dresses. Girls ran and ran.

Leonardo da Vinci asked if they wanted to make something. Kids were screaming.

Amelia Earhart asked if anyone would like to fly a plane. Men and some women followed her.

The boy asked if he could play. His mother said yes. First he went to Walt Disney. He made a movie about the hole. It was called *The Sunny Day*. Next, he went to Roald Dahl, he also wrote about the hole. It was called *The Five Lucky Birds*. Finally, he went to Leonardo da Vinci. He built the hole. All he thought about was the hole in the sky. At night he said to himself, "Why is there so much banging?"

The next day it was sunny. The five people wanted time to themselves. So, everybody else got to enjoy their day. That night the hole was there. The five people said goodbye, then they went up the hole. A second later, they were gone. And so was the hole. That night, it was nice and peaceful. No banging. Everybody got a good night's sleep.

The End

Some creative art work will stand on its own. The teacher of the poet below thought that the following poem written by a tenth-grader deserved wider attention, although he failed in helping that student find publication.

I Was at Peace by Beth Wine

I was at peace . . .
When I awoke this morning
Hearing the birds chirp
The breeze blow
And the sunshine warm

I was at peace . . .
Until I felt the bed
Not of clover, but springs
The birds chirping
Not free, but in cages
The breeze blowing
Not thru treetops, but the window

And it wasn't the sun at all . . .
Just the electric blanket on "high."

I was at peace
(When I awoke this morning)

Goodbye
Goodbye for now
Goodbye for tomorrow
Goodbye forever
Goodbye

And as you go
I'll give you . . .
A kiss for luck

A kiss for life.
And one for love

I'll godbless you and
The road you travel
I'll hope you travel the same road
Back to me.

Goodbye

AN ARTIST'S VIEW ON HOW SCHOLARSHIP AND RESEARCH INFORM ART

Artist Ty Pownall helps clarify how creative scholarship involves the understanding that the scholarship grows out of a history of having studied with masters and research in terms of looking back at both the history of art and looking back at previous uses of one's chosen materials.

Ty writes:

> Art, whether primarily experiential or referential, is a product of its contributing predecessors, constraints within the moment of creation, and estimations of the future. Considering predecessors, one should think of both the work that has come before and the direct academic instruction from "masters." In my own art practice I simultaneously build on and oppose my instruction as well as the art canon. A single example of both of these is my examination of the language of Minimalism. In my recent loose sand works, I'm creating simple geometric forms that can reference landscape, architecture, and the iconic geometric forms of minimalist sculpture. Considering the forms of Donald Judd and Carl Andre but constructing them in loose sand allows for a vulnerability that I feel links our current moment in history to similarly precarious times in the past.

Pownall well explains how his work depends upon his own scholarship and research, as well as how snugly he fits within its ecology.

THE THOROUGHNESS OF CREATIVE ART AS SCHOLARSHIP AND RESEARCH

The example of Pepperdine University undergraduate drama student Dino Constantine suggests that it is no stretch to think that the work of artists can involve as much or more thorough research and scholarship than even that of the scientist. Remembering that the word "research" means "to look again," and that the original meaning of "scholar" was "one studying with a master," student-actor Constantine conducted a massive amount of research and scholarship on his way to playing the lead in the Pepperdine University Drama Department's staging of the musical *Les Misérables*.

More than a year prior to the casting for *Misérables*, the musical was announced as being on the horizon as a Pepperdine event. An actor, but not necessarily a vocalist, Constantine undertook a year's worth of voice lessons to prepare merely to audition for a singing lead. (If he had failed to be given the role, would that have diminished his scholarship?)

From casting to the final performance, his research was ongoing and extensive. Constantine studied with the musical's director, an acting coach, a musical coach, and a choreographer coach from rehearsal to final performance. He also studied former productions of *Misérables*; he read and studied Victor Hugo's novel *Les Misérables*; he read histories of the times; he read criticisms of both the original novel and previous renditions of the musical production.

He also studied his own performances, both introspectively and in conjunction with the others in the cast. The amount of research and scholarship toward a very limited number of performances was extensive. The amount of time he spent might be compared to that of the student living in the science lab at a well-known medical school who is pursuing both an MD and a PhD.

Both the lab rat and the obsessive-compulsive theatre major evidence remarkable dedication and persistence. Well-done science and art require research and scholarship.

M. Norvel Young, a former president of Pepperdine University, often remarked in regard to such comparisons that "there is no competition among lighthouses." One need not compare an inspirational series of performances to incremental findings in a science laboratory. However, one can justly recognize the depth of research and scholarship that can go into both.

HOW SCHOLARSHIP AND RESEARCH INFORM CREATIVE ART

Creative artistry, at least in academia, consistently involves scholarship and research. The student studies with a master and that master ordinarily has an academic degree that evidences that this teacher also studied with a master (invoking the traditional definition of scholar). Pepperdine University's renown classical guitarist Christopher Parkening studied with Segovia. In a discussion with a few of Parkening's students, one student remarked, "I look back on past masters' interpretations as a starting point." Another reported (with reference to both Parkening and Segovia), "I have two great sources to take from."

Reportedly, such creative advice "certainly shows up in a performance in terms of how the different aspects of playing are prioritized." The student mentioned such aspects as the technical, tone; and musical, interpretation—

including playing things on different places on the guitar. The complexity, rigor, scholarship, and research that goes into a performance is comparable to the work that goes into the forms of research and scholarship associated with the sciences.

RECOGNIZING CREATIVE ART OUTSIDE OF FINE ARTS— EISNER'S THE TEACHER AS ARTIST

Ralph Beck was a beloved teacher and basketball coach. Demanding but fair, he did it so well his results had aesthetic qualities. Whereas the elementary school play cited elsewhere may have been better assessed by the criteria associated with action research, the depth of Beck's work might be better understood by applying criteria associated with aesthetics. Elliot Eisner (1979, 153–55) identifies four senses in which teaching can be an art, and this applies to Beck's coaching. He coached with great skill, he made judgments that unfolded during the course of both practice and games, he used a qualitative form of intelligence that seemed unique to him.

His activity was never dominated by prescription or routine. His ends were often created in process. No one ever saw Beck taking notes or gathering data in any systematic way. The artist has a different way of researching. Beck had great perception about people and about the game of basketball. He seemed to soak up everything that was going on, catching details others would have missed. And then he acted.

This too is important action research, and its results benefitted each student under his charge. For Beck, delivering a presentation, or writing a paper or book, would have been superfluous to his main interest. Sometimes deep respect from those who know you trumps any wider acclaim.

Looking for criteria that fit is more important than judging by set criteria. As a teacher and coach, Beck was an artist.

COMMONALITIES OF ART AND SCIENCE IN KEY TERMS

The first examples above establish that in a general sense artists and scientists have much in common as scholars and researchers. Eisner has written extensively about those commonalities.

The watchwords in academia of the past decades have included *empiricism*, *research*, *scholarship*, *rigor*, and *robustness*. While these words have been associated with scientific approaches to knowledge, in fact the terms especially apply to all academic work.

Empiricism means "based in experience" and as such equally includes science and art, and teaching-learning at all ages.

Research means to "look again," which also applies to science and art, and all students and teachers.

C. P. Snow (1959) wrote about the two cultures in academia: science and art. *Research* has historically been most associated with science. Tom Barone and Elliot Eisner argue that the "processes engaged in by many artists make it sensible to call their work research" (Barone 2012, 47). They offer the following definition of research: "Research is, yes, a process of *re*search*ing*—that is, of coming back again and again to perceived phenomena, scrutinizing the world, then thereby re-experiencing it" (Barone 2012, 47).

Elliot Eisner, Stanford University professor and former president of the American Educational Research Association, worked mostly from artistic paradigms. He argued that artistic paradigms are also *empirical* because they are also based in experience. He argued that artistic paradigms are *research* oriented because *rechercher* means to look again—that is, to study, and nonnaive art does just that.

He also relied on the anthropologist Ernst Cassirer to argue that only with both art and science do we get *bifocal* vision, and thus depth perception. Thus the terms *empiricism* and *research* meaningfully account for most academic work from kindergarten onward. At the very start of school, students engage in experience and then in looking back at that experience.

Creative scholarship/arts-based research and scientific research complement each other. Together art and science form a complete ecology of research and scholarship.

Scholarship originally meant to have studied with a master, which tends to remind one of working with an artist even more than a scientist. "In the English-speaking world, the word scholar first appeared in the eleventh century, with a strong social component. Scholarship, according to the Oxford English Dictionary, was not seen as an isolated activity. A scholar of that day was typically a student who was training or had trained with a particular master. By the sixteenth century, the term applied to one who had acquired learning in the schools . . . the historic definition of scholarship supports an inclusive appreciation for what all professors do" (Glassick 1997, 62).

By that definition, any student work that has been supervised by a teacher entails scholarship.

If at least historically, scholarship is the work with a teacher, there are many faces to scholarship: traditional research done in natural science; traditional research done in social science; the kind of research done in the humanities and religion most often includes library research. Business and communication can be expected to have students who have done research based in social science methods. *Expressive* work, especially done in fine arts, creative writing, screenwriting, journalism, filmmaking, and so on also entails scholarship in the work with a "particular master." Scholarship thus also potentially includes instrumental and vocal art, acting, photography, exceptional journalism, exceptional debate, and so on. Students of all grades and ages participate in such work according to their developmental stages.

Robustness can mean "energetic, well argued, not easily disproved." "Indeed, robustness can be viewed as the underlying mechanism leading to complexity" (ianswers.org). Certainly some art, like some science, distinguishes itself with its visible robustness.

Rigor. Science is to be celebrated for consistently demanding a standard of rigor across all forms of inquiry. But the conscientious artist laboring with the palette to obtain the exactly right color, hue, brush stroke displays work no less rigorous. "In research, rigour is defined as the quality or state of being rigorous, valid, credible, grim, believable and thorough. It also means being harsh but just or true in action and treatment. Rigour is being strict in conduct, judgement and decision.. . . When done well science and art invoke standards of rigor because rigor is defined as valid, credible, and thorough. It also means just or true in action and treatment. Rigor is being strict in conduct, judgment and decision. It is thorough and exacting, complex and meticulous" (ianswers.org).

When done well, science and art invoke standards of such *rigor* because rigor can be viewed as the underlying mechanism leading to complexity.

The argument here is that the gamut of all work undertaken by students, teachers, and educators is empirical, inherently based in research and scholarship, and informed by the standards of robustness and rigor. A working definition of scholarship could well be "that work undertaken by scholars."

Qualitatively, creative scholarship demands an uncannily comparable degree of empirical effort, research, scholarship, robustness, and rigor as its more prosaic and scientific counterparts.

Creative scholarship and arts-based research both involve research and scholarship. They both make vital contributions to the ecology of any learning community.

Together, art and science, scholarship and research, provide the depth perception necessary for understanding.

A note: Having argued for an inclusive appreciation of research and scholarship, such academic work should still be distinguished from naïve scholarship. Although not always easy to identify how academically based creative scholarship and arts based research are *scholarship*, such work is at least implicitly informed by an academic background. Andy Warhol's work was informed by his understanding of art history. This was much less, or not at all true, for the still highly regarded art work of his contemporary, Basquiat.

The commonalities of scholarship and research with artists and scientists do not mean that they share common standards for appraisal.

Eisner elucidates how the criteria for scientific forms of inquiry are different from those for artistic forms.

The criteria for appraisal . . . Scientific approaches to research ask whether or not the conclusions are supported by the evidence, and further, whether the methods that were used to collect the evidence did not bias the conclusions. In other words, scientific research is always concerned with question of validity. For a research study to be judged valid, a variety of criteria need to be applied to it. There range from appraising the character of sampling procedures and the magnitude of instrument reliability to the less tangible areas of interpretation.

In artistic approaches to research, the cannons of test reliability and sampling do not apply. While one might question a writer's or film producer's reliability, there is no formalized set of procedures to measure writer reliability; one doesn't really want the mean view of four writers' observations about the mental hospital in Oregon which served as the subject matter for Ken Kesey's play. One simply wants Ken Kesey's view. Its validity, if that is the appropriate term, is to be determined by our view of its credibility, and not by reducing his work to some average by using only that portion that it shares with the views of others. Validity in the arts is the product of the persuasiveness of a personal vision; its utility is determined by the extent to which it informs. There is no test of statistical significance, no measure of construct validity in artistically rendered research. What one seeks is illumination and penetration. The proof of the pudding is the way in which it shapes our conception of the world or some aspect of it.

(Eisner 1981, 6)

Eisner's four ways in which a teacher becomes an artist (see Beck above) and his criteria for appraisal (just above) suggest criteria by which to evaluate creative art. Take the poem by Beth Wine printed above.

In terms of the artist, did she:

1. Show skill and judgment?
2. Evidence a qualitative form of intelligence?
3. Engage in the creative process?
4. Avoid prescription and cliché?

Yes, to all four.

In terms of the work, did she:

1. Communicate a credible wistfulness of a felt emotion?
2. Offer a persuasive personal vision?
3. Write a poem that informs?
4. Create a work of illumination?

Yes, to all four.

There remains the qualitative judgment about the degree of her success in those eight criteria. This poem goes well beyond what might be expected of a tenth grade student. Her poem has artistic success. Teachers certainly want to encourage such creative artistry among young scholar-researchers. However, a different set of criteria for appraisal are probably much more applicable for evaluating most student efforts.

How does an elementary school administrator evaluate the quality of a well-rehearsed play put on by the elementary schoolchildren? A marble game was central to the performance. Who would have thought that the dramatic lead would pick up marbles from the game's circle with his toes as he delivered his lines? Can the drama teacher be held responsible for such bad acting? Yet virtually all of the planning and decision making that goes into *serious* theatre was operant. How does that administrator evaluate the aesthetic qualities of the performance?

The criteria Gary Anderson and Kathryn Herr (1994) cited previously for practitioner research fit better than aesthetic criteria. The work on the play was *collaborative* with the students. The outcome was *valid* in that the play was presented to the student body, all lines delivered. The process was validated in that *appropriate preparations* were made from casting, to rehearsal, to performance. The overall experience had *catalytic validity* in that the students were energized to participate and wanted to do another. And in terms of *dialogic validity*, much discussion ensued by cast members, other students, teachers, administrators, parents . . . with more than some good humor in terms of the audience appraisal of the students' performances.

John Dewey wrote that the purpose of criticism is the reeducation of perception. In evaluating any effort of scholarship and/or research, appropriate criteria must be matched with the object of scrutiny. In an educational setting, all work is preparatory. Simultaneously, students should become gradually aware of the criteria for art and science at its finest, while being evaluated on educational criteria matched to developmental needs.

In terms of the themes of this book, the example of the elementary school play has greater import than more accomplished examples. Art should be for everyone.

It is potentially an empirical question. Ask kindergartners to raise their hands if they are artists and almost all will raise their hands. By junior high school, perhaps no student will raise a hand. When was the change? Why? What went wrong? A student should not have to be good at music or art to benefit. Where would Nobel Prize Winner Bob Dylan have been if he'd paid attention to what is taught about music and its performance in school? One of the Beach Boys' high school music teachers was once interviewed on television. He had reason to recall, drolly, that he had given a *C* to a song that a Beach Boy had written for his class. The song went on to sell several million copies.

English teachers study literature. By using presumably great examples they also tend to create the impression that such work is not something that students can do. At least in most art classes students still get to paint. The standards of fine art are out of reach of almost all students. But who knows how much richer lives would be if everyone kept creating?

Creative art is not only for specialists.

Ernest Boyer emphasized the importance of diversity within the professoriate; might this not equally apply to some amount of diversity within the individual scholar's career? The very word research means to look again. Elliot Eisner points out that both artists' and scientists' work are empirical in that both are based in experience. Within a career, a professor of painting might very well profit by writing a peer-reviewed article, and the social scientist by painting a cognitive map, if only for herself.

Painter Marc Chagall's *I and the Village* might very well inspire a teacher's commitment to creating a learning community. Fine art inspires in different kinds of ways. Professors are more likely than K–12 teachers to have opportunity to display juried work. But surely fine art deserves a place in the K–PhD curriculum beyond the isolated course? Surely many more teachers can find a place for artistic expression?

How will that work be evaluated? In rare, exceptional cases, send it somewhere for publication, competition, public viewing. In most instances the criteria for arts-based research (in the next chapter) may be more helpful.

Creative artistry increases human understanding.

Chapter Five

Arts-Based Research

I've always been inspired by artists who have shown musical and intellectual curiosity and the courage to take risks.
—Renee Fleming

Arts-based research can at least seemingly differ from *creative artistry* because of its potential difference in focus. Certainly the argument can be made that all art is political, and certainly artistic success is not always a matter of technical superiority. Nonetheless, it is useful here to recognize the historical argument of a painting that may be said to be "Art for Art's sake," versus a line drawing used by educator and philosopher Paulo Freire for work with literacy in South America.

Freire's art work was evaluated on its educational significance, on whether it created *dialogics* about generative social issues. While the art in arts-based research has to be somehow good enough, the educational aims have a greater claim in evaluation. As another form of scholarship and research, arts-based inquiry needs a language for such evaluation.

The emphasis is on the educational significance of arts-based research with a requirement of only artistic adequacy.

ARTS-BASED RESEARCH AT ITS FINEST

Tom Barone and Elliot Eisner (2012) suggest that the artifacts of arts-based research can approach or even become art. Sarah Attar's arts-based research serves as an impressive case in point.

Sarah Attar was the first woman from Saudi Arabia to run in the Olympics. A Pepperdine University student, she later created a self-portrait in conjunction with a Seaver undergraduate research project. Her arts-based research was informed by the Olympic torch. She superimposed a photo of the torch over a photo of her face. Her art professor, Gretchen Batcheller, authoritatively spoke to the image's aesthetic success. But the resulting self-portrait involved not only creative scholarship, her effort was also arts-based research. She explored from a political/social/educational/psychological/sociological perspective, through the medium of photography, the theme of identity. Her work was born of experience. Her study was rigorous in its meticulous and exhaustive study of her experience, the press coverage of her Olympics participation, and her library research, as it all pertained to the issue of identity. Her study was robust in its complexity on many different levels.

Hers was not only Art for Art's Sake. Her photography provided insight into cross-purposed influences that impact personal identity: arts-based research.

THE FAILURE TO RECOGNIZE ARTS-BASED RESEARCH

Filmmaker, author, and professor Craig Detweiler made a documentary film, *Purple State of Mind*. Craig had done an MFA in film at the University of Southern California, and studied theology with, among others, Rob Johnston, author of *Reel Spirituality*. In ways perhaps more difficult to describe, Detweiler's film was suffused with techniques learned at USC and ideas influenced by a mentor, Rob Johnston. In this film, Craig and his former roommate at Davidson College conducted the kind of research associated with its historical definition of looking back. They looked back at personal histories and religious history, seamlessly stitching them together into the film.

Detweiler's subsequent book, also titled *Purple State of Mind*, was written for a wider audience than a strictly academic one. The extensive chapter notes at the end of the book are a testament to the scholarship and research that undergird the film as well as the book. Craig's time spent on the film and book was vast, and an important use of a professor's time. Somehow he managed to get tenure despite the fact that neither of these examples of scholarship and research were considered scholarship or research in the Rank, Tenure, and Promotion review.

Pointedly, Craig is not complaining. He understands that is how the system has been working, and he made his accommodations. This is, nonetheless, extremely unfair to the recognition of his very real and important research. The ecology of scholarship and research demands that professors have the latitude, at least some of the time, to pursue their greatest interests.

Eisner (1998, 1) argues that "seeing, rather than mere looking, requires an enlightened eye: this is as true and as important in understanding and improving education as in creating a painting." He says further that "the Enlightened Eye is about the perception of qualities, those that pervade intimate social relations and those that constitute complex social institutions" (Eisner, 1998, 3). This work seeks to meet his expectation that the educational critic has the aim "to help others see and understand."

Detweiler's work is important scholarship and reached an audience in ways that even his book could not.

UNINTENDED CONSEQUENCES OF ARTS-BASED RESEARCH

Heuristic sacrilege.

He wondered how was it that apparently no one had updated Raphael's painting *The School of Athens* to *The New School of Athens*. The professor of literature and philosophy, realizing that a picture was worth a thousand words, updated fifty of the faces of Raphael's painting of ancient Greek philosophers at the entrance to that academy. The updated theme: literacy. Oprah, she of the famous (or is it infamous?) book club, replaced Plato. Said professor spent more time on the selections of new, contemporary faces, and on the potentially heuristic implications of the selections, than on a typical scholarly article.

Judge the results for yourself (http://newschoolofathens.wixsite.com/pepperdine). But on what basis will you judge? The substitutions of faces did not aspire to Art. The poster was created to have educational significance for the students in the College's Great Books program. The students had to create their own icon as a final capstone response to their two years in the Great Books Colloquium. The teacher felt obliged to create his own icon. Some thought it a penetrating look at literacy. Others thought it disrespectful to a great work of art.

Undoubtedly he was a senior professor. Who else would have the gall to try to use the vehicle of satire to communicate the study of an educational culture?

He would laugh aloud as he wrote a handbook for his students—an obvious sign that he was not nearly serious enough to be undertaking anything of educational significance? As Michael Apple (1977) revealed, by kindergarten students learn the difference between work and play, and that school is work. Hard work. Even dreary work. If it doesn't taste bad, it must not be good for you. Einstein marveled that "it is a miracle curiosity survives formal education."

The professor was reading through historical enchiridions by Augustine, Erasmus, Epictetus, but also historical Boy Scout handbooks, and even his granddaughter's copy of the handbook for Jedi Knights. He had the audacity to conclude that an educational culture was inducting its students into a very specific educational identity, and that that identity deserved scrutiny.

Criticism is tough enough to take, but satire? Only students laughed at the results, and not quite all of them. The students, of course, knew they weren't supposed to laugh, and that something was awry with this new *Enchiridion*. Nonetheless, some of those students were not yet sufficiently socialized to stifle themselves. And one student claimed that reading the handbook was the major reason that he had moved from the bottom to the top of the class. Such creative scholarship has great worth if only for a limited number of one's own students.

Naturally the powers that be were less forgiving. The five steps of the scientific method, a proper literature review, T tests, and the universal conclusion that more research is required should have been the order of the day.

If the professor wanted to validate that students connected the faces with the issues of literacy, further evidence would be gathered. Meanwhile, the effects on the person conducting the research matters. His *New School of Athens* captured many of his otherwise ineffable feelings about literacy.

THE CRITERIA FOR ARTS-BASED RESEARCH

Here is an example of scholarship that demonstrates the potential of using an established set of criteria to explain the meaningfulness of an innovative research project.

Pepperdine University Professor Joi Carr creates a *Multicultural Theatre Project* production each year. Students audition for the performance, but they need no prior theatre experience. They rehearse for a semester, but the emphasis is on the content of each separate part of the production. An individual show might include dance, spoken word, one-act drama, song, video productions, art work, poetry, and so forth.

The individual parts are carefully put together into an organic whole that communicates the diversity and the richness of the multicultural experience, through literature and historic texts as the framework for the production. Professor Carr chooses each part with the care an artist uses in choosing different colors from a palette. Early in her academic career, her work was recognized only as service, instead of the arts-based research that it is. Fortunately, that injustice has recently been repaired. The criteria for arts-based research by Barone and Eisner were a brilliant match for an assessment of Carr's production of *Lift Every Voice*.

Barone and Eisner (2012, 148) identify six criteria for arts-based research.

- Incisiveness
- Concision
- Coherence
- Generativity

- Social significance
- Evocation and illumination

Utilizing these criteria, and the language of Barone and Eisner, for an evaluation of Carr's *Lift Every Voice* reveals the rich success of the production. The overall script certainly got at the heart of the complex Civil Rights and social issues (*incisiveness*) of the King era. The collage/kaleidoscope/montage/impressions/segments were remarkable in "occupy(ing) the minimal amount of space and least amount of verbiage necessary for it to serve its primary, heuristic purpose of enabling members of an audience to see social phenomena from a fresh perspective" (*concision*) (Barone and Eisner 2012, 149). The immediacy of the performers and the currency of the issues belied the historical distance.

With regard to *coherence*, Carr created "a work of arts-based research whose features hung together as a strong form" (*coherence*) (Barone and Eisner 2012, 150–51). The individual pieces were variations on a common theme. There was a multiplicity of responses to the Civil Rights movement. With regard to *generativity*, the work enabled one to recognize and potentially act upon phenomena that involve justice and civil rights. The work anticipated the "Black Lives Matter" issue that later surfaced.

The show was also successful in terms of *evocation* and *illumination*. This is "important because it is through evocation and illumination that one begins to feel the meanings that the work is to help its audience grasp" (Barone and Eisner 2012, 153). The production realized the *social significance* of the past in relationship to the present.

With such a variety in performances, the audience was prodded to wonder why no live singing was included. The spoken word was used in most of the individual segments. One answer would seem to be that this placed a greater emphasis on the *content* more easily being understood by the audience. This choice had the effect of balancing the rational and emotional. The intensity of the performances was balanced by the clarity of the spoken script. Thought and feeling merged.

The material was already sufficiently emotional. Causing the audience to focus on the texts that included countless spoken lyrics, insured a certain intellectual distance. That perspective heightened a deeper appreciation of the very emotional issues. Carr's arts-based research indeed "got to the heart of a social issue" (Barone and Eisner 2012, 148) surrounding the era of Dr. Martin Luther King Jr. Very few of the cast and audience members had been alive at that time. Seemingly everyone left with a better understanding of the past. The halcyon call was then to leave the auditorium, to think about what had been experienced, challenged to lift personal voices founded in a tradition and legacy that bespoke the steep price of freedom.

Two other perspectives speak particularly well to the importance and significance of the arts-based scholarship associated with Carr's multicultural theatre project. Philip Jackson emphasizes the upward direction of the scholarship of discovery, but that teachers are necessarily focused, then, on the downward view of the teacher toward the student. While professional *juries* of artistic work are undoubtedly worthwhile, the larger point may be missed—the only essential criteria should be how the selected material impacts the participants and their audiences.

Even the most novice participants rose to the occasion and communicated earnestness, seriousness of purpose, emotional involvement, perhaps humility, in repeating words that had been so expensively spoken in the past. The event was a profound experience for participants and the audience. This is overwhelmingly what was most important about the event.

Second, the Eisner quotes below suggest that no one has done any important teaching or scholarship until it has been completed emotionally. *Multicultural Theatre Project* does that. Anything less is incomplete teaching and incomplete scholarship.

In his *What is Education?* Philip Jackson (2012, 43) observed,

> The experts were chiefly concerned with the abstract structure of knowledge (what we have been calling its essence), whereas teachers' concerns are more divided and somewhat more mundane. Teachers are certainly concerned with the structure of knowledge, as are the experts, for in the end that is what they aim to conserve and transmit. But they are also concerned with how that knowledge rests with those they teach. To that end, they are often called on to be judgmental about what their students say and do. That is where the pedagogical manifestation of rectifying and expanding finds its place.
>
> In coming to terms with the embryonic and imperfect state of their students' knowledge, teachers almost invariably face a mixture of right and wrong. I call that condition existential simply because it exists, not because it has any profound philosophical meaning. It is based on experience and can be empirically verified by testimony, but its imperfection calls for modification. Essence and existence await separation. Yet, oddly enough, they also beg to be unified, if not at once, at least in the long run. Immediate pedagogical intervention is required, even though its ultimate goal in some ideal sense may turn out to be unreachable.

Carr's theatre program, utilizing classic texts and student performances, certainly "unified" experience and knowledge.

This unification was both empirical (based in experience) and imaginative—a quality true for both science and art. As Eisner (2002, 198–99) observed, "Educator and Professor, Philip Jackson, has written about the *essence* and *existence* that of imagination in science is revealed in the work of Nobel laureate Barbara McClintock. To get a sense for the organism, as she called it, McClintock employed her imaginative processes to participate empathetically in the interior of a living cell." The student performers clearly used their experience "to participate empathetically" in the Civil Rights Movement's texts, and in a scholarly and imaginative way.

Eisner continues,

> John Dewey once commented that the stamp of the aesthetic needed to be on any intellectual idea in order for that idea to be complete. It is this feel, both imaginative and sensible, that the so-called academic studies would foster if they were modeled after the arts. John Dewey had something to say about the relationship of the intellectual to the aesthetic. It is this: "What is even more important is that not only is this quality a significant motive in undertaking intellectual inquiry and keeping it honest, but that no intellectual activity is an integral event (is an experience), unless it is rounded out with this quality. Without it thinking is inconclusive. In short, esthetic cannot be sharply marked off from the intellectual experience since the latter must bear an aesthetic stamp to be itself complete. (Eisner 2002: 198–99)

Undoubtedly, Carr's students' performances emotionally completed the work begun in their intellectual research.

While professional *juries* are undoubtedly worthwhile to establish the high quality of the production, the larger point may be missed—the most essential criteria will be how the selected material impacts the participants and their audiences. Second, as suggested by the Eisner quotes, no one has done any important teaching or scholarship until it has been completed emotionally. The multicultural theatre project does that exceptionally well. Anything less is incomplete teaching and incomplete scholarship.

The scholarship and the experience of *Lift Every Voice* were deeply meaningful and commendable.

Arts-based research demands sufficient aesthetics as to be comprehensible and workable, but its overriding concerns are heuristic and must be evaluated accordingly. Such arts-based research has the potential of contributing to completing educational experiences in all disciplines. Carr's work is a remarkable example of a scholar's arts-based research.

Chapter Six

The Scholarship of Service

> To disclose to the world something which deeply concerns it, and of which it was previously ignorant, to prove to it that it had been mistaken on some vital point of temporal or spiritual interest, is as important a *service* [emphasis added] as a human being can render to his fellow creatures.
> —John Stuart Mill, *On Liberty*

> Life's most persistent and urgent question is, "What are you doing for others?"
> —Martin Luther King Jr.

The school had a work day. Students K–PhD need service opportunities. Frank was in a small group asked to rid a parking lot of weeds that had crept up through cracks in the asphalt.

There were three hoes for the five volunteer workers. It would be hard work. The boys would be glad to share.

The weeds were indefatigable.

The hoes became instruments of mass destruction.

Which worked for a while.

Then, one by one, the hoe handles broke from the stress well before the job was complete.

Service opportunities are important, and they need to be well conceived.

The English teacher drove a school van for a food can drive. Students went door to door asking for food donations, particularly canned food, for the city's food banks. Certainly language arts skills were required. But it was hardly why the English teacher or students were involved.

This new teacher was more than a little surprised to find that every year the poorest students from the poorest school collected the most food from the poorest neighborhoods in the school district. How was that possible?

The teacher has now thought about that question for fifty years.

He still has no definitive answer.

School-related activity beyond the classroom has the great potential of stimulating questions, some of which invite further academic pursuits.

And some that are just worth thinking about.

Our professional language is only beginning to catch up to how the scholarship of service is integral to scholarship and research.

Hector had been truant. Ostensibly he was in tenth grade, but in reality he had been AWOL. Now he was tutoring fourth-graders in reading. Hector actually read slightly below his own grade level. But he was well above the fourth-grade level.

Hector had enrolled in the district's experimental school. One of the school's expectations was cross-age tutoring. Service learning.

The look in Hector's face when he returned from his first tutoring experience with fourth-graders was rapt.

When he first enrolled in the program, Hector's face was blank, listless. When he returned from tutoring fourth-graders, it was like an inner light had been turned on. He was excited, animated, purposeful. He could hardly contain his enthusiasm. Outside of school, in fact, Hector was a great kid. In school, he had been frustrated, angry, and eventually despondent. Helping a fourth-grader was transformative. One could see it on his face. Instead of sitting passively in class, he had helped someone. It was a supremely good feeling. A fourth-grader had looked up to him. It was magical.

Hector looked forward to the tutoring. He also improved immensely as a student.

Service learning can have powerful general results for a young scholar. And in the terms of this book, Hector's was an act of both scholarship and research. He could help a younger student because some of his teachers had been successful in teaching him to read. He was a scholar in that he had studied successfully under teachers. He also looked back at his own experiences, especially his frustrations, in researching how he might be effective with a younger student. Such an opportunity increases understanding in untold ways.

The student-created website minimally represented a scholarship of service. It was definitely informed by its academic interests. It was organized according to the usual areas of faculty evaluation: scholarship, teaching, service. The site housed exemplary academic work created by students, but the site itself was not an example of academic content. But students were able to review each other's work there and that had academic value.

Areas of scholarship overlap. The key is to avoid standardization, and to appreciate conscientious and successful academic work, whenever and however it appears.

The Korean American administrator who earned an EdD from a prestigious university collaborated with a professor of education from one of his alma maters. The Korean American administrator/scholar had written his dissertation on issues about the benefits and costs of stereotypes of Korean American students in school.

The study was about the hidden curriculum, and how the apparent advantages that Korean American students accepted from ostensibly positive stereotypes worked against those students with the highest educational aspirations. The study had potential (service learning) import for students, like this Korean American scholar had been. The journal on Asian American educational issues rejected the article because it purportedly reinforced the stereotypes by having studied them. The specious rejection also meant one less publication for career evaluation.

John Dewey wrote that the purpose of criticism is the reeducation of perception. The person engaged in the scholarship of service would do well to find the connoisseur who can provide the insightful criticism necessary for a fair evaluation.

Elliott Eisner and Tom Barone, both proponents of connoisseurship and criticism, recommended that arts-based research be evaluated in terms of *concision, coherence, generativity, social significance, evocation,* and *illumination* (Barone and Eisner 2012, 148). These terms can be effectively applied to service learning.

In education, perhaps no one has met such criteria applied to service learning better than Paulo Freire (1970), and the work he did with social literacy.

Freire's team created drawings that elicited dialogue among students. The pictures elicited generative words that led to both literacy and social literacy. As such, the drawings certainly "occupied the minimal amount of space and least amount of verbiage necessary (to) serve its primary, heuristic purpose" (*incision*). The set of drawings established the key themes (and *coherence*) of the students' lives. For example, a drawing of a man with a mule at a well elicited conversation about the relationship of nature to civilization, and elicited further conversation about what it meant to work the land.

The key vocabulary thus identified became truly *generative* as the words led to full literacy. The *social significance* was sufficiently impressive, and Freire so successful in working with marginalized citizens, that he was forced to leave two different South American countries. The *evocation* and *illumination* were such that Freire and his *Pedagogy of the Oppressed* became arguably the most influential book of educational philosophy of the second half of the twentieth century.

Certainly, other works of scholarship of service will not likely have the long-term effects of Freire's work, but this example tends to show the potential efficacy of using the criteria of incisiveness, coherence, generativity, social significance, and evocation and illumination to evaluate works of scholarship of service.

Having suggested in the vignettes only some of the problems associated with giving proper recognition and credit to service, what about the professor asked to spearhead service learning? How could that professor ever gain due respect within the rank, tenure, and promotion system? How would a review committee evaluate the scholarship?

What is the academic worth of having influenced professors across the college to add service-learning opportunities to the curriculum? What is the academic worth of working with groups of students to create tutoring work in reading for local schools? What is the academic worth of having worked with students and professors to do volunteer work in women's shelters? What is the academic worth of having coordinated hundreds of student volunteer efforts?

How might service learning be assessed, measured?

If one were to count the New Carnegie Units (appendix) this would be one of the hardest working members of the faculty. But couldn't this work have been done by a staff member? Not really. The faculty status gave credibility to the university's goal of building service into the expectation for undergraduates. The faculty status gave the professor the attention of other professors.

Being on faculty committees enhanced the probability of service opportunities for students and faculty. The faculty status made it possible to include service learning as part of the curriculum. The faculty status made it much more possible to apply for grants. The faculty member also created a viable academic program complete with objectives, readings, structured learning activities, and methods of assessment and evaluation. Curriculum development is an acknowledged act of scholarship. The faculty status improved everything except an obvious way to be evaluated according to traditional expectations for faculty members.

After all, would not a grant for further service opportunities be more important than an article? Would not being one of the few to stimulate collaboration across all academic areas of the college be more important than membership in a prestigious educational association (when an appropriate one does not yet exist)? Would not the service of hundreds of people be more important than the service that this person might do independently?

The lesson: eschew standardization—set high standards. The criteria for a scientific journal are mostly straightforward. The criteria for recognizing the quality of scholarship for service probably need the *criticism* of a *connoisseur*. There is no competition among lighthouses. Bob Dylan need not be compared to Pavarotti. Basquiat need not be compared to Picasso. Fred Astaire need not be compared to Nuryev. But when it comes to rank, tenure, promotion decisions, some qualitative decisions demand to be made.

A major intent of this book is to create more appreciation of the necessary diversity of the teaching profession and some empathy for those struggling with less traditional, or at least less traditionally acknowledged, forms of scholarship. A colleague bemoaned, "I have been told that I would never get tenure because of my work. . . . I have been told (that my work) is 'common sense,' 'meaningless,' and 'not academically rigorous.'"

No good deed goes unpunished. Responses to such discouraging words vacillate between "virtue is its own reward," and Henry Beale's, "I'm mad as hell and won't take this anymore." Maybe if colleagues had started learning the skills of colleagueship in kindergarten . . .

PART OF THE DIFFICULTY OF EVALUATING SCHOLARSHIP OF SERVICE

The service opportunity could have hardly been more poorly conceived. Two dozen college students and a young college professor ventured into Mexico under Project Amigos to build a children's hospital in Tijuana. The college students had virtually no construction skills. The building for the hospital was smaller than a middle-class home in neighboring San Diego. It was being built out of the materials used in the most modest of those US homes, cinderblocks.

The hospital that was being built did have the advantage of being, besides the nearby church, the only other solid building, the myriad of homes in this poverty-stricken area being made of nailed-together plywood, advertising signs, and discarded roof shingles, above dirt floors. The hospital walls were going up, and there was yet no sign of plumbing.

That the homes received their water from cisterns mounted on flatbed trucks that visited the neighborhood each day dispensing water was a strong indication that there would be no indoor plumbing for the medical facility. That the hospital building was more substantial than the surrounding homes perhaps would offer some hope for the prospective new patients?

The building site was adjacent to a cemetery. All day long, a procession of funerals wailed the loss of loved ones. Could this new hospital have staved off some of those deaths? Many of the burials were of tiny coffins. The respective mothers gave full voice to grief, sobbing and screaming in ways that made the US college student volunteers uncomfortable at best, and somehow troubled whether in conscience or spirit.

These college volunteers had ample time to observe these funerals because they mostly stood around. Without any construction skills, they mostly moved cinder blocks to where they were needed, and occasionally did a bit of clean-up work.

No indigenous people were involved in the building project.

The college students and professor slept each night in the home of someone in San Diego. Because of the numbers of college students and the lack of any other parents of the college students who happened to live in San Diego, most experienced the discomfort of sleeping on the floor.

One of the students had driven to Tijuana in his old Plymouth. He invited four others to take an adventure into the tourist section of Tijuana to buy bongo drums, or leather sandals, or dirty pictures—whatever would be the most suitable souvenir from the excursion. He did not mention to the group that he had lost one of his contact lenses and he was having some problems with his depth perception. He did not speak nor read Spanish. Thus, when he inadvertently turned the wrong way into a one-way street, he quickly realized his error but misjudged his U-turn and bumped a small temporary building where bottles of different liquids were sold to tourists.

The students jumped out of the car to make sure nothing had happened to the vendor in the building. To their shock the one person behind the slipshod counter was breaking bottles as fast as he could. Increasing the damage to what purpose? What was that all about?

Within seconds, a gendarme was running toward the accident. Tales of spending time in the infamous Tijuana jail ran through college-aged minds. Whether no one ran because they were so conspicuously out of place and would quickly be apprehended, or whether it was to stay and support their friend, the driver, well, who was to say?

Fortunately, one student in the group of five who was not white spoke a bit of Spanish. Arrest was clearly not what was being discussed. Money was the issue. Quickly, the students came up with all the money they carried. The total amount of cash did not meet the policeman's original asking price, but apparently it was enough. In front of them, the policeman then split the money with the vendor, and the students were allowed to return to their work at Project Amigos.

Back in San Diego, the student found it difficult to sleep that night. He happened to be placed on the den floor next to the college professor who had accompanied them. The student asked the professor about the worth of the trip. They had not worked with any Mexican workers. They accomplished so little in what was only a very inadequate hospital building. Each night they fled back to the United States side of the border. It didn't seem all that worthwhile.

The college professor confessed similar criticisms of the effort. But he said that it was worth his while to be with this group of students and that one may never know the payoffs for such undertakings.

Hopefully that college professor received credit for his college-related service. He went because he was asked by students who would go on to advanced degrees including in the area of health and medicine. The professor was a political scientist. If he had been the instigator of a service project that would take students to Mexico, he certainly would have conceived something much more efficacious.

This Project Amigos trip had been planned entirely by students. The professor was not asked to consult, only accompany. He did so with good humor, even slept on the floor, and while obviously observant, made no criticism. Students experienced the evidence and consequences of their work, or lack thereof, individually and personally. Perhaps the professor went on this ill-conceived journey simply because he was afraid he might otherwise have to travel to Tijuana to bail some of his favorite students out of jail.

On the basis of any program objectives, the trip to build a hospital was very poorly conceived. Even if medical help was eventually given out of this very shoddily built building, the college students' time was very poorly and inefficiently used. Any list of usual assessment criteria would find this project severely wanting.

The daily observance of the poverty, with the return to the relative comforts of San Diego each night, just as likely reinforced any prejudices about ethnicity, social class, and even religion, instead of having challenged such prejudices.

A major danger would be to assume that service projects are primarily to serve. Service projects are very often primarily to learn, especially when undertaken with students. If only because of age, students have a limited range of experiences. Especially to appreciate educational theory, students need what John Dewey refers to as a necessary "funding of experience."

Even if the student who spoke critically to the professor about Project Amigos had actually had a few construction skills and had been able, for example, actually to use mortar to build the cinder blocks into walls, the contribution would have been a very modest result compared to the time and effort and even money to get there and work a few days.

For at least that one college student, the cultural shock persisted for a very long period of time. Arguably no one likes pity, or benefits from pity. At least as commonly understood, pity invites condescension. But eventually shock was replaced at least by some small amount of empathy. One serves because one desperately needs to learn more from service learning than one can actually contribute to said service.

Educators have long known that one never really knows the outcomes. Objectives and assessment criteria might have been helpful in the design of a better project for Amigos, but any short-term, or for that matter, even long-term, measure of purported educational outcomes can never get at the long-term influence and consequence of students working together and with a teacher.

While the service project may have had fairly dismal results in terms of what it contributed to friendship between the United States and Mexico, limited evidence suggests that the project created enough cognitive dissonance among the participants that much was going on in what Benjamin Bloom and associates identified as a taxonomy for learning in the affective domain as well as the psychomotor domain. Donald Clark (2015) describes that the affective domain "includes the manner in which we deal with things emotionally, such as feelings, values, appreciation, enthusiasms, motivations, and attitudes."

The Project Amigos effort might well have been what Dewey identifies as a miseducational experience. The experience in Tijuana may have reinforced cultural prejudices and cut off future such humanitarian efforts on the parts of the students. While much more might have been hoped for in the intentional plans for service learning, the program did succeed at the "receiving phenomena" level on the affective taxonomy. That affective domain includes five major categories. The first is the *receiving phenomena*. It involves an "awareness, willingness to hear, selected attention." Even students discussing the program's failures led the students to "awareness, willingness to hear, selected attention."

Service learning entails research and scholarship. Assessment and evaluation demand research and scholarship. One way or another both involve the affective domain—critically important, critically neglected. The same can be said for the psychomotor domain.

The unplanned, inadvertent car accident during Project Amigos yielded the highest level of psychomotor performance (and perhaps learning). "The complex overt response" rests at the highest level of the psychomotor taxonomy. Clark (2015) provides the description of this category as "the skillful performance of motor arts that involve complex movement patterns. Proficiency is indicated by a quick, accurate, and highly coordinated performance, requiring a minimum of energy. This category includes performing without hesitation, and automatic performance."

The five college students had had previous complex problem-solving experiences, but responding to the specific problems of a traffic accident in Tijuana, Mexico, required extremely quick thinking and problem solving while under extreme duress. The group had mere seconds to negotiate an unfamiliar language and the unprecedented personal experience of police corruption.

While it is understandable that schools of higher education emphasize the cognitive, affective and psychomotor learning is taking place regardless and can be instrumental to a full sense of the scholarship and research involved.

While the cognitive outcomes of service learning may be difficult or impossible to assess at the end of a service learning experience, the usually neglected affective and psychomotor domains deserve and demand attention. This is often where the most important learning takes place and is replete in service research and scholarship.

Service learning deserves full respect for its social significance and its scholarship and research. Perhaps the criteria proposed by Eisner and Barone for arts-based research can be adapted as well as attention to both the affective and cognitive domains as sources for significant teaching-learning experiences.

The last line of the Pepperdine University affirmation is "that knowledge calls, ultimately, for a life of service." The mere fact that virtually all schools of higher education are nonprofit organizations speaks to the implicit and explicit idea that they are intended for the social good. Surely for university-supported service to be meaningful, it has to be based on informed ideas. The argument here is that service is so central to the mission of higher education that it merits an esteemed place in the categories of recognized scholarship.

Perhaps the greatest misconception of service is that the primary benefit goes to the person served. Quite probably students are asked to sit and listen to superstar servants who have been asked by those in charge to share their stories as guest speakers. Quite probably those same students react by thinking that since they do not yet have their own lives together, they certainly do not have anything to give to others.

A young teacher in northern California, one of a very stable, even privileged background, found herself teaching in an inner-city school. Whatever contributions she may have made to her students, she reports that she benefitted far more. She found direction and purpose. She learned about herself. She learned to appreciate differences and to diversify instruction. She thinks she became a better person.

Any academic evaluation of service needs to recognize that the greatest benefit may go to those offering to serve.

Invidious comparisons among forms of scholarship invariably lead to proponents of the less prestigious forms to feelings of isolation and even despair. The argument here is that the necessary diversity in teaching-learning makes for the healthiest learning community and the most generative overall research and scholarship. Affirming that knowledge calls, ultimately, for a life of service makes a claim on establishing a scholarship of service.

Chapter Seven

Curriculum Development, Administration, Community, Colleagueship

> Human spirit is the ability to face the uncertainty of the future with curiosity and optimism. It is the belief that problems can be solved, differences resolved. It is a type of confidence. And it is fragile. It can be blackened by fear and superstition.
> —Bernard Beckett

Teachers need not do all the heavy lifting with curriculum development. At the beginning of each new unit, teacher extraordinaire Gene Bream would ask students to bring in anything that they had that might pertain to the upcoming unit. Grandparents, diaries, photos, films, friends, souvenirs, and so on consistently add depth and texture to each unit.

Elsewhere in this book, John M. Daly was lauded for his work in Advanced Placement and Honors History, Alice Coleman for her work with Advanced Placement and Honors English at Mission Bay High School in San Diego. They were teachers in the early years of Advanced Placement in America's high schools. They were quite probably the first in their urban school district to gain approval to teach their respective courses.

They worked in tandem. They convinced their principal to schedule their Advanced Placement and Honors classes back to back and to have the same students for both junior and senior years. This would have the impact they sought. Their students started getting into better and better colleges. Graduates would return to extoll the virtues of working as hard as Coleman and Daly demanded. For a host of reasons, such curriculum development involves scholarship and research and has the potential to change students' lives.

Uh-oh.

The high school vice principal attributed much of his success in school when he was a student to his love of sports. From a very early age, he read the sports section of the newspaper and sports stories in magazines and books. He not only read voraciously, he learned to do baseball statistics, which inevitably helped him with his school math. He thought that what had worked for him might work for some high school students.

Serving as summer school principal, he created and gained approval for a sports literature class that could count as an English requirement. He recruited a teacher who also loved both English literature and sports. He felt confident that the sports literature class would attract students to summer school. And it did. Sort of.

While the course was not a complete failure, it fell far short of hope and expectation.

The class attracted roughly three kinds of students—maybe three students who were enthused by the subject, about fifteen who had failed English that year, and about fifteen more who thought that since the class was about sports it would be easier than the usual school offerings.

Pretty much the whole class thought that the sports literature stories were just as boring as the ones they usually had to read in their normal English classes. It was a great course—for some other students. One of the cardinal rules in the scholarship of curriculum development is to match plans with students, or court disaster.

The education professor who taught the reading class had been a big fan of the read-a-long format as a child. His daughter had also (these were the olden days) put on her head phones and listened raptly to read-a-longs on long car trips. This professor was persistent. He even convinced George Lucas to provide written transcripts of the NPR radio series of Star Wars programs for the read-a-long experiment.

The professor determined to do a fairly traditional scientific study with an experimental group and a control group. Although the groups ended up being too small to have as high a T-score indicator so that the results were solid, the students in the experimental group improved their reading scores to twice that of the control group. Impressive.

Impressive? Read-a-longs simply do not fit the way teachers can best organize groups of thirty or more students. No matter how promising the innovation, it will not impact school classrooms if it does not fit into the ways teachers must necessarily organize teaching. Does that diminish the quality of the effort? These students profited from this curricular innovation.

The question remains. What will be the relationship of research and practice?

THE POLITICS OF CURRICULUM DEVELOPMENT

In 1986 the college had no film courses. The division chair in the Social Sciences Division determined to remedy that. Elliot Eisner schooled his students to look for what was missing and the absence of film study seemed to be a void.

The Humanities Division sent a letter suggesting that it was not appropriate to have a film class in the Social Sciences Division, even though the one course in film that they used to teach was no longer in their curriculum. The Communication Division sent a committee to meet with him, telling him that a film class did not belong in the Social Sciences Division.

He prevailed by having the course titled A Social Science Perspective on Film. A few years later he was able to gain approval for a film minor. The minor included the courses Religion and Film, History and Film, A Social Science Perspective on Film, and Asian Films. Later still a film major was adopted, a major quite different from what the Social Sciences Chair had originally had in mind for film study.

The Chair thought that the best way to study film was like the study of education. Scholars from a variety of academic disciplines like history, political science, philosophy, literature, psychology, sociology, and so forth would turn their focus on the study of film. Such could be a beneficial way of approaching film study.

However, the emerging field of film studies had a different view.

Film study would become an independent field like math, or English, or economics. With the development of film schools, film studies became its own discipline with its own unique assumptions and methods of inquiry.

The concern here is not which view of film study was better. The observation here is how ideas and initiatives take on a life of their own in the ecology of education. Understanding how scholarship and research work hopefully informs the work on curriculum development. Despite its complications, or because of them, curriculum development is an act of scholarship and research.

Alas, despite having a PhD from a major university in general curriculum, the professor realized that not everyone reviewing his vita would recognize curriculum development as an act of scholarship. Thus he wrote another professor at another university who had graduated from the same doctoral program. He had had similar frustrations. He responded: "When we became teachers, who knew that we would be educating our department chairs and colleagues!"

In education, curriculum development is a recognized act of research and scholarship. In fact, as education curriculum scholar Bruch Uhrmacher states: "Curriculum development, implementation, assessment, and evaluation are all well recognized as scholarship in the field of Curriculum."[1]

Certainly in education, all curricular work is informed by a professional research literature. In fairness, shouldn't curriculum development in other fields also be recognized to some extent for its research and scholarship implications?

Perhaps Ernest Boyer is correct in his belief that all professors should evidence the ability to do original research at some point in their careers. Surely there should be a premium on scholarship of discovery. But that is no excuse for failing to appreciate the workloads of other professors who devote much of their research to teaching, and who also benefit the whole in a pronounced way. All the forms of research and scholarship inform academic work.

SCHOLARSHIP OF ADMINISTRATION

The Preface credited his high school teacher John M. Daly as an influential teacher. Daly taught Advanced Placement History and Honors History because the principal of his school had a special appreciation for scholarship and research.

That principal replaced the teacher who had been at the school longer, who had been teaching those courses, and who even had a doctoral degree, with the Princeton-educated Daly. In the context of working with a high school faculty, which ordinarily prizes seniority and longevity, it must have been a courageous decision. The principal must have had an idea of the importance of how this teacher from the Ivy League could better prepare young scholars as researchers capable of success at top-tier colleges.

Administrators may no longer be in the classroom, but their practices and policies remain based in their understanding of scholarship and research. Their decisions influence the institutional scholarship and research.

A tenured professor was not getting the job done in the classroom. What administrator but a scholar would be qualified to oversee the evaluation of the respective demands of tenure that protects academic freedom versus the responsibility to students in the classroom?

Each decision made by an academic administrator has great import for all the other forms of research and scholarship: which grants for reassigned time will be given, how much of the budget will be for professional travel, will all forms of scholarship be equally weighted for rank? For tenure? For promotion? Will travel funds for student travel be at the expense of funds for faculty travel? What will be the class sizes so that instruction is balanced with teaching? Will the *best* professors be scheduled in lower-division courses to interest students in the field, or to provide advanced students with the most specialized teaching?

How often and toward what ends will the curriculum be assessed? Redone? What will count as course substitutions, if any? Will guest speakers be chosen to confirm or to challenge the dominant paradigms? What are the implications of the necessary diversity among teachers? Are those teachers who are most flexible when it comes to meeting short-term needs for covering a variety of courses punished in terms of promotion?

School administration may be the most underappreciated form of research and scholarship. Certainly, administration requires the scholarship of service, assessment, evaluation, and curriculum development. If this is not true, professors would not expect, even demand, that administrators with authority over academic matters be chosen from their ranks.

If this is not true, nonacademicians could be hired, returning valuable professors to the classroom. Intuitively, professors know that a businessperson, lawyer, or office manager cannot serve as the academic chair, or dean, or provost. If academic decisions are to be made, firsthand understanding of research and scholarship is required. In turn, such decisions are based in research and scholarship.

The practicality of defining scholarship as the work that can only be done by a scholar becomes especially evident with regard to administration. A new faculty hire requires a relooking at the history of a program and school: the students' needs; any current gap in faculty expertise; the candidates and school in terms of potential fit. Such decisions must be based in academic sense and sensibility.

A student sought a contract major in the liberal arts. He was from a well-connected family and was most insistent that the collection of courses he had taken in liberal arts was sufficient to qualify as a contract major, except that he had no rationale whatsoever for how his collection of courses met any definition or rationale for a liberal arts or humanities major. This Chair needed, and needed to look back at, the history of the liberal arts major in higher education to adjudicate the conflict and come up with a suitable academic plan.

A faculty member proposed a new minor in women's studies. Early on in this history of curriculum change in higher education, such a proposal was controversial. Women's studies was not a traditional academic discipline. What would be the field's knowledge base? What would be its methodology? The administrators needed academic expertise to negotiate this evolution in the curriculum of higher education.

The administrators needed an appreciation that the university curriculum had already evolved far beyond the original seven liberal arts of the quadrivium and trivium, and how applied fields like agriculture, business, education, communication, and so on had become a part of the curriculum in higher education. Academic administrators need an academic background, and hopefully some wisdom, to realize the claims of emerging areas such as film study, ethnic studies, women's studies, ecology, leadership, and so forth for inclusion in the curriculum.

Hopefully, academic administrators have had the opportunity to have already proven their scholarship of discovery chops, and dedication to other appropriate forms of scholarship. The New Carnegie Unit (appendix) might then be used to indicate whether there was any other available time for still other forms of scholarship, including the need to recognize the importance of the scholarship of administration.

EXTENSION/CONTINUING/COMMUNITY SCHOLARSHIP

Basil Bernstein's conceptualization of *classification and frame* (1975) offers a helpful way of understanding why most scientific scholarship earns more academic prestige than any scholarship of service. It is a matter of *boundary conditions*. The *code* that holds together scientific disciplines has much *tighter* boundaries than what are oftentimes referred to as the *soft* approaches to knowledge. There is so much agreement among scientists that the knowledge they create is often considered *objective*. Under such conditions it is easier to gain recognition that a new work represents set, readily identifiable standards.

When anyone does an act of service, who could ever know its full importance? A professor at a private college was asked by the local school board to participate in an ad hoc committee toward the creation of a new high school. The proposal for the new school was extremely controversial. The new school would serve one of the wealthiest areas in the district. Although students from anywhere in the district could potentially enroll in the proposed new school, the major reason for creating it was due to how difficult it was to navigate the traffic to get to and from that geographical area.

The ad hoc committee, representing a number of constituencies from the community, met regularly for a year and filed a report recommending the creation of the new school. The politics were such that a large majority of the communities served by the district were hostile to the proposal. Nonetheless, and somewhat surprisingly, the district school board voted to adopt the proposal and create the new school.

There was a subsequent rumor that inside deals had been made, and that the professor on that committee would be the next superintendent of the district.

How might that professor's act of service be evaluated within the context of rank, tenure, and promotion? That a professor was on the ad hoc committee lent a certain academic credibility to the work of the ad hoc committee. But it would be difficult to identify specific ways in which the final recommendations of the ad hoc committee were based on any expertise that came from the professor's academic discipline, even though it was education.

The high school was created and has since served many hundreds of students. Yet these students were in a school that had much less diversity than the school district as a whole. But then again, as traffic conditions only worsened over the years, more and more of the students from this wealthy community would undoubtedly have opted for private-school education that was more readily accessible.

The net effect of this loss of students within the district would have severely affected the general revenue that served the entire district. Furthermore, there is no reason to have thought that the decision of the school board would have been different with or without the participation of this professor. (She certainly did not go on to become an administrator in that district.) How might this professor's community-oriented scholarship best be evaluated? With difficulty, but that does not make it impossible.

COLLABORATION AND SCHOLARSHIP

The colleagueship and collaboration of Larry Giacomino, Charles Park, David Holmes, Craig Detweiler, Joi Carr, James Thomas, Stella Erbes, Christopher Parkening, Joe Piasentin, Ken Montgomery, Sally Bryant, Ty Pownall, Gretchen Batcheller, Sonia Sorrell, Regan Schaffer, Alexis Allison, and Jordan Hess made this study possible. Their time was valuable and somehow such contributions to others' scholarship is also an act of scholarship. Such generosity has a generative effect in the overall ecology of research and scholarship.

NOTE

1. Bruch Uhrmacher, e-mail correspondence with author, September 29, 2009.

Chapter Eight

Scholarship of the Student

The mind is not a vessel to be filled, but a fire to be kindled.

—Plutarch

STUDENTS AS TEACHERS

The first-year teacher was being observed. It was an unannounced visit. Fortunately, the class was engaged in small groups answering questions about short stories. Midway, the teacher stopped the class to clarify an issue. A group of five sitting in the back corner next to the observer whispered to one another during the teacher talk.

The teacher was tempted to scold the group, but worried about handling a discipline situation in front of an observer. He resisted the temptation and ignored the whispering. Those students could be dealt with later.

At the end of class, the new teacher waited for the observer to criticize him about discipline. The visitor opened the conversation: "I was impressed by how engaged your students were. The small groups really worked. For example, when you used a word the students didn't understand, the student who knew the word told another student and they passed the information along to each other."

"Oh."

The students who learn course content earliest reinforce that learning by teaching it. Students can also be effective passing it along to others in the same class.

Cross-age tutoring works well for giving students teaching experience. But such a practice has proven difficult to arrange on a regular basis. Small-group discussions and projects within the classroom have two distinct advantages. First, students read each other better. They are more likely to recognize when another student has failed to understand. Second, they are more likely to use an appropriate vocabulary to explain things. Sesquipedalian transmitters of knowledge may eschew obfuscation, but still prefer polysyllabic etymology.

Two potential downsides to such student work need to be monitored. An unengaged student may remain unengaged. Students are more likely than the teacher to mis-explain a course idea. Nonetheless, involving students in teaching has many benefits.

A STUDENT BECOMING AWARE OF CONFLICTING IDEAS ABOUT SCHOLARSHIP

The literature student researched what the scholars had already had to say about Gerald Copley's poem "The Groundhog." That student went on to become a professor. What she remembers most about her undergraduate study of this poem was that the best review of that poem had been written by a professor who reported that he had hated the poem the first few times that he had read it. The definitive review of the poem had been written by someone who had hated the poem to begin with?

In that era the focus was supposed to be on strictly analyzing a poem. Yet this reviewer had included biographical detail in explaining a relationship to the poem. Not only were there apparently no rules for literature professors, one could not necessarily trust one's own initial readings of a work. Perhaps it was the difference Jane Austen intended with her title *Sense and Sensibility*? Perhaps sense depended upon proper sensibilities? The critic's discovered thought about the poem stemmed from pondering an emotional reaction. Such a distinction is a studied example of the necessary scholarship of the student. Students learn about academic attitudes as well as academic knowledge.

One need not dismiss emotion in scholarly work. In fact, such emotion likely points toward a fruitful line of inquiry.

SOMETIMES IT IS THE WORK CONDITIONS, NOT THE SUBJECT MATTER

Was the tedious work calibrating thermostats to measure ground temperature the best possible preparation for significant scholarly work in geology? Certainly, as with any field of study, the willingness in this case actually to roll up one's sleeves and do the grind work was a critical part of what it took for success in the field.

Thus was it an educational or mis-educational experience? In that particular year, no lab assistant went on for graduate work in geology.

MONTY PYTHON WENT TO OXFORD, CAMBRIDGE, AND OCCIDENTAL

The young Advanced Placement high school students knew that they were required to substantiate their research with well-chosen quotations. However, it was not always possible to find just the right quotation. Unless . . . the group known as Daly's Five created their own book, *Gosuphal's Quotable Quotes*. When they needed a quote they could always write one themselves and add it to their book, footnoting it appropriately.

Having some fun with ideas likely contributes to a student gaining enough distance to see the forest instead of the trees.

CRITICAL THINKING IS A REQUIREMENT FOR STUDENT SCHOLARSHIP AND RESEARCH

The doctoral student was working on a research team investigating the effects of the Progressive Movement on New York City schools. This aspect of a larger study involved looking at a pictorial study of those New York City schools as revealed in the school district's publication of its annual reports. One year, the report revealed a school-district commitment to traditional education. The representative picture was of a classroom of about thirty students who all had smiles on their faces, hands eagerly raised to answer the teacher's question, from desks that were in very tidy rows if only because they were literally nailed to the classroom floors in neat, tidy rows.

Suddenly in the very next year's report, students were outside on field trips and working in groups at various places on campus. The year's report was enthusiastic about the commitment to the progressive ideals that suddenly had currency.

The doctoral student had been a school administrator. Her experience had been that schools change slowly . . . and that it would have taken an inordinate amount of time to transform all those classrooms with the nailed-down desks into work areas. But the yearbook's rhetoric and the visual evidence was that within one year New York City schools had gone progressive.

She looked at the doctoral advisor with a look of incomprehension. The advisor, a noted educational historian, simply returned the gaze, but seemingly without any expression whatsoever. The doctoral student started and stopped several times in trying to explain the sudden transformation to progressivism, and then literally sat back in the overstuffed leather office chair, while keeping keen eyes on the face of the advisor.

It became an *aha* experience. The light bulb went on instantaneously. She suddenly blurted out, "They changed superintendents and they took different pictures." The doctoral advisor smiled broadly.

Historical interpretation apparently comes much more easily to those who have enough background in the subject to do what Ernest Hemingway referred to as crap detecting. The student had much to learn and it was not only about the discovery of knowledge. There was also a scholarship of learning, a scholarship of the student.

WHICH STANDARDS APPLY TO STUDENT SCHOLARSHIP AND RESEARCH?

Madison, an undergraduate communication division filmmaker, was not very impressed with fellow student Mason's *Inebriated on Great Books* video take on Dostoyevsky. Madison invoked the aesthetic and technical standards of her film major. Mason's film icon, however, had noteworthy educational significance. A student could write a scholarly paper on Dostoyevsky's *Notes from the Underground*. Elliot Eisner argues that a student should be able to respond academically in other iconic forms.

Mason's film was an unusually apt response to Dostoeyvsky in a more novel form. While not otherwise a schooled filmmaker, he created a video that captured the interest of the other students in the class, demonstrated that he clearly understood the book's main themes, and emotionally made Dostoyevsky's book his own. He was notably successful by the expectations of student scholarship.

A painting student, a creative writing student, a journalism student should be recognized when s/he produces a particularly robust/deep/insightful work based in the sensibilities of a formal education . . . but a student not majoring in those areas should be able to use the format of a film, a painting, a short story, dance, sculpture, and so forth for academic exploration. The criteria should be its educational significance and its heuristic intent, rather than simply the artistic merit.

Mason's artistry was good enough, his educational success remarkable.

While advocating experimentation with forms of scholarship and research outside of one's comfort zone, humility and the search for apt critique would insure greater clarity. A social studies teacher in an urban school heard his students' complaints about the school lunches, and that they were less in amount and nutrition than the guidelines for school lunches. He had an interested handful of students take on a research effort. Indeed, they found that the lunches they analyzed fell short of expectation, mostly because of portion size.

However, they only analyzed five lunches a day for five days. The serving sizes were irregular from lunch to lunch; some made the grade; but on average they did not. The school newspaper covered the scandal. Certainly some of these students bought a lunch that was less than advertised. But they had such a small sample size that it would be impossible to determine whether this was a general problem.

They identified a problem, gathered some data, weighed the meals accurately, but with such a small sample size this may or may not have been a random versus systemic problem. Certainly at least one low-wage staff member working as quickly as possible might have been well advised to find a different method of allotting portions as the trays were swiftly filled and passed along.

The encouragement here is to undertake scholarship and research of all kinds. Those skills need to be honed and developed, but also with an eye toward the limitations of any study.

A student, Jim, who was remarkable for such student scholarship was asked, "What is, or will be your best piece of scholarship? Are you doing a senior thesis for example?" He answered: "I am doing a senior thesis; however, I expect my best piece of scholarship will be a philosophy essay I wrote last year that I am shopping around to get published. I wrote it for an ethics class and Dr. B. helped me revise it into something suitable for publication."

He was asked, "What are some examples of 'studying' studying you have done? Can you give an example where you were studying the process of being a better student as compared to directly studying the subject of your class?" He responded, "The only 'studying of studying' I have done is trial and error over the years. By that, I mean I observe and discuss with my classmates the methods they use and then try them out. If it worked, in that I felt it allowed me to retain the information I needed, or organize the information sufficiently well to write an essay or something, then I use it again. For example, I used to use flash cards, but then discovered multipage, color-coded study guides were more effective in helping me memorize things."

He was requested to identify as specifically as possible some of the things he had done that showed his service and colleagueship were directly related to the official school curriculum (as compared to the cocurricular like fraternities, intermurals, clubs, etc.).

Jim responded, "I'm a fan of collaborative studying. I take good notes and make my study guides as soon as is appropriate, and then let it be known that if anybody wants a copy of either I'm happy to email them. I organize study groups to go over ideas. Talking things out helps me cement concepts, so I try to organize study groups so that we can talk everything out, answer each other's questions, or resolve conflicts in understanding. Though this doesn't relate exactly to the curriculum, I try to keep the atmosphere fun and light because I think that the right atmosphere, namely one that is interesting and welcoming, will encourage us all to work together and participate."

The student's answers evidence an implicit understanding of the demands of the scholarship of the student. How can the teacher best help all students to emulate his initiative and scholarship of the student?

APPLYING CRITERIA FOR PROFESSORS TO EVALUATE STUDENT WORK

Curiously, scholars are primarily associated with the content that they teach. Traditionally, scholars have a fourfold responsibility: certainly for research in their subject, but also teaching-learning, service, and colleagueship. Given that the original meaning of "scholar" was to have studied under a master, any role modeling or mentoring of students suggests that the same fourfold responsibility applies to the students as well. A scholar's student would presumably engage in learning, research, service, and colleagueship—all four. How could it be otherwise?

A professor of a California college taught a course run as an experiment. This professor wondered why the preponderance of courses taught in college were organized as if each student was going on to specialize in that subject. In fact, quite probably not one of those students, statistically speaking, would be likely to go on to earn a PhD in that subject. However, IF the premise was to prepare each and every student to continue toward an advanced degree in the course's subject, why weren't those same students also socialized as if they were going to go on to become teachers/professors of that very subject?

Instead of grading the course on the basis of quizzes, exams, and term papers, the students of this course were offered the option of being treated like faculty members in an institute studying the subject at hand. The students were to be evaluated qualitatively in the common collegiate areas of scholarship, teaching, service, and colleagueship. Each student by the end of the term completed a *faculty data form* based on the work undertaken that term, and were peer evaluated according to the rubrics of scholarship, teaching, service, and colleagueship.

As part of the study, and perhaps to ensure a fair amount of participation, students were also to keep logs of their time spent on the course, cataloging their efforts by time spent on such activities as reading for the course and time spent on an academic project (whether that project was a paper or some other form of academic scholarship). Each student was invited to teach a part of at least one of the classes that term.

Fourteen students chose to take the class. Excluding the student with the highest grade-point average going into the class and the student with the lowest grade-point average, the middle twelve students had an overall collegiate grade-point average (on a four-point scale) of 3.7. This was a very responsible and talented group of students, many of whom the professor thought might be strong candidates for future doctoral work and perhaps careers as professors.

At the course's completion, this professor thought that good work had been done by each and every student. The surprise was that the very best work was done by the student with the lowest overall undergraduate grade-point average, nearly a full point lower than the class's average. Not only was this student the leader of the group that created the most impressive work, this was also the student who put in three to four times more work than any other student. This student also elicited the best collaborative work in the class, and evidenced the greatest intellectual curiosity. She set the highest standards for the quality of work. Her commitment to finishing a quality project was—whatever it took.

Philip Jackson coined the term the *hidden curriculum* to describe how the lessons in school are often more in how one is socialized than what academic knowledge one might learn. Elliot Eisner observed that schools most often teach compliance. James Herndon wrote that schools primarily separate the sheep and the goats. Ostensibly those students who do the best academic work in the context of a school class are those most socialized to continue in school.

The general pattern is that the very best students distinguish themselves on teacher-constructed assignments all the way up to a thesis or dissertation, and then, suddenly, with little precedent for such an expectation, that same student is expected to work strictly from an independent locus of control and create an original study, without class support, without deadlines, without any kind of exam on the topic.

Wouldn't a preferable way of sorting and selecting those who go on to become professors call for academic courses to be organized according to those students who have their own agenda, can work collaboratively, work from an internal locus of control, go above and beyond usual expectations?

Despite the limitations of this single, informal experiment, it would seem worth pursuing the possibility that at least some academic classes should work from the prototype of how actual college professors conduct their work, and how they are evaluated.

WHICH STUDENT WAS THE BETTER STUDENT BY FACULTY CRITERIA?

Given the need for future scholarly professors, the lack of attention to student scholarship seems surprising. Certainly, among the fortunate few who are apprenticed by professors in a mentoring relationship, the four areas (scholarship, teaching, service, collegiality) where professors are evaluated has at least the potential of spilling over into expectations of students.

Occasionally an individual class may exceed expectations. Sometimes that may be due more to an individual student's effort than that of the teacher. Certainly, the research suggests that what the students do is even more important than what the teacher does for learning. In the Fall of 2013 at a private, West Coast, undergraduate college, students outperformed the professor's expectations. Certainly, her first hypothesis was that she had simply done an even better job of teaching than usual.

More likely the add-on results were due to a budding scholar in the class ranks. One particular student, not necessarily the best student, assumed a leadership role. In terms of performance on both the midterms and final exam, this student had only the second-highest score in the class. In this class on teaching, the student who scored the highest was content simply to do her own work.

The student who placed second took the lessons (and research) on teaching and learning to heart. She knew that the research suggested that the best way to learn something was to teach it. She was also especially idealistic and motivated. She took it upon herself to rewrite a midterm into a model midterm to share for other students' benefit. She set the bar for classroom presentations by offering to do the first one, and doing it thoroughly and imaginatively. She held study sessions before the final exam for those interested.

The student with the highest score in the class and this student who took great responsibility for the class peer group both had the talent to become scholar-professors. The second, however, best evidenced the range of skills necessary for being a well-evaluated faculty member. Not only did this second student use critical course concepts analytically, she also demonstrated remarkable colleagueship, service, and teaching.

Research indicates that there are advantages and disadvantages to students explaining course concepts to other students. The potential downsides include that such students are more likely to be somehow wrong about the ideas. Reticent students may also be reticent in engaging peers. Nonetheless, the potential advantages include that students use more appropriate vocabulary for explaining ideas to other students. Also, students read each other's body language more accurately in determining whether the receiving student is, indeed, comprehending.

Quite probably the academic success of this class as a whole was due to the combination of the efforts by the teacher and this student-teacher (without diminishing the due credit to each student and their own individual work). This potential professor also accrued the benefits of experience in the teaching that is required for future professors.

Directly related to the teaching was the implicit and explicit act of service. Setting up study groups outside of class hours was a notable service. Not all college classes end up having study groups. Student initiative is required. On rare occasions, students may enhance their own learning and provide an important service by tutoring lower-division students in subjects that are prerequisite to the subject at hand. Other courses find students doing volunteer work in related ways within the community. Such service has value within itself. Such service also prepares budding professors for these career expectations.

Finally, this student who helped others succeed in the class was well regarded by the peer group for her colleagueship. This is revealing. After the first midterm, which had had very mixed results, the students were polled by e-mail on whether they would like an additional practice midterm before the final exam. The student who had scored the highest responded that "I do not." That was a completely reasonable personal preference. The faculty member reported her exam to be one of the finest ever received for a midterm.

The student who finished second, however, responded that she thought a practice midterm would be helpful for the class as a whole. Such concern suggests a greater priority for the values associated with colleagueship.

Academia rightly recognizes the best academic performance of students regardless of issues of colleagueship, service, and teaching when it comes to a letter grade. However, academia might do well to encourage all students to develop these skills even if they are above and beyond the academic performance that gets graded.

John Dewey suggests education/learning/scholarship is not complete until it has made an emotional connection. Philip Jackson argues for the unification of the essence and existence. Knowledge needs to stand a test of time by being passed down from person to person and generation to generation. Any scholarship of discovery necessarily requires both a scholarship of teaching and a scholarship of the student.

When it comes to student scholarship, two related but separate considerations deserve special attention. First, like the scholars supervising their students' work, efforts of unusual quality, depth, and insight deserve special recognition. Whether an individually designed experiment, an exceptional write-up of an aspect of a larger study conducted by the supervising professor, a very high-quality painting, a journal article of both depth and awareness, such student accomplishment should be recognized at least as formative examples of research and scholarship.

Second, while knowledge for knowledge's sake and art for art's sake will always have the most esteemed position in any taxonomy of scholarship, efforts by either professors or students that have particular *educational* purport or import also merit special recognition. For example, while professors may engage in the scholarship of teaching, presumably students anticipate such scholarship on their own parts by engaging in the scholarship of study.

Young scholars gradually develop skills in the areas of scholarship and research, teaching and learning, service, and collegiality.

Chapter Nine

The Legacy and Ecology of Education

> I could not, at any age, be content to take my place by the fireside and simply look on. Life was meant to be lived. Curiosity must be kept alive. One must never, for whatever reason, turn his back to life.
>
> —Eleanor Roosevelt

The professor was attending a student's doctoral dissertation defense. He had occasion to remark on one of the academicians being discussed. The candidate asked the professor where he had learned something about the seemingly ancient scholar being discussed. The professor smiled, nodded, and said in something of a whisper, "He told me."

One should not undervalue the educational legacy passed down person to person.

Scholars are not rock stars. At least in the olden days before the Internet had older people more worried about their privacy, the dissertation writer called public telephone information and asked for a home phone listing for the extremely influential Harvard scholar. The scholar was listed in the telephone directory.

The student called. The phone was answered. The conversation was sufficiently stimulating that the California student flew to Boston for a personal interview. That is also part of the excitement of scholarship, and making an emotional connection with the knowledge and the new research. The scholar's generosity toward the student substantiates the too-infrequent emotional connection that sustains and generates scholarship across generations.

The normative conventions of social science research make a lot of sense. Standard deviation finds that most sets of data group around a common mean with a preponderance of cases falling within a standard deviation of that mean. But what about the outliers? What about N=1? A PhD kind of doctor went to a medical doctor about plantar fasciitis, a very painful condition in the arch of the foot. The doctor gave the advice that would fit almost all cases—"Don't even go to the shower without wearing orthotics."

The pain persisted, and the patient wondered how much his arches might hurt if he weren't wearing those orthotics.

But his son-in-law, who was a hospital administrator, and who, perhaps, had a more reasonable understanding of doctors, suggested that the father-in-law visit the local Shoe Doctor. The "Shoe Doctor" was called that by his clients. He was only a shoe salesman, and he was not comfortable with that honorary title, but . . . this high school graduate, who was also a runner, and who consulted with untold numbers of other runners about shoes, asked the supplicant to walk in the store. He observed. He asked the customer about how long he had been wearing orthotics. For years.

The Shoe Doctor's prognosis was that the patient had not been flexing his arches for so long, that that might be the problem. This person in such great pain, who had been religiously wearing his orthotics and suffering through his pain for nearly three years, decided to take the advice and to go without the orthotics every other day. His pain lessened immediately. After he dispensed with the orthotics altogether, the pain went away.

Unlike most others with plantar fasciitis, this person needed to flex his arches without orthotics. The problem with normative data is that it is not very helpful to the outliers. Eventually each part has to inform the whole. Scholarship relies on its own intricate, built-in biofeedback. What generally applies to the whole does not necessarily apply to all of the parts. A healthy ecology reacts healthily to exceptions.

Over time the best ideas are handed down. The legacy can be passed along institutionally or personally. John Dewey had retired from Teacher's College Columbia by the time Philip Jackson became a student there. Apparently the spirit of Dewey still roamed the halls. Here is the publisher's blurb (University of Chicago Press) on Jackson's book that indicates that he was inspired by decades of thinking about Dewey:

> One day in 1938, John Dewey addressed a room of professional educators and urged them to take up the task of "finding out just what education is." Reading this lecture in the late 1940s, Philip W. Jackson took Dewey's charge to heart and spent the next sixty years contemplating his words. The stimulating result of a lifetime of thinking about educating, *What Is Education?* is a profound philosophical exploration of how we transmit knowledge in human society and how we think about accomplishing that vital task.

Philip Jackson was one of Elliot Eisner's professors at the University of Chicago. At Stanford University Professor Eisner would often assign Jackson's *Life in Classrooms* (1968) to his doctoral students. Eisner (1979, 198–99) also brought the philosopher, Ernest Cassirer, into the discussion of *binocular thought* (science and art) in education. Eisner expanded his thoughts on Cassirer by referring to the work of one of Cassirer's own students, Suzanne Langer. Langer, an aesthetician, argued that *discursive* language was inadequate for the expression of feeling, and that *nondiscursive* alternatives were required. Eisner used ideas from John Dewey to clarify his understanding of educational *connoisseurship* and educational *criticism*. Scholar to scholar, institution to institution, excellent ideas are passed along.

An essential quality of a healthy ecology of research and scholarship is the passing along of the best ideas. Hopefully such ideas were sufficiently understood as to have contributed to this study.

Educator and professor Philip Jackson (2012), has written about the *essence* and *existence* that is involved in education and hence scholarship. He argues that the polarity demands unification. On the one end, scholars discover knowledge, come up with theory. But that scholarship is not complete until it is realized in the particular. Students and teachers are responsible for matching theory and practice.

Dewey argues that knowledge is not complete without an emotional connection to that knowledge. For example, at the *Great Books Pnyx* at Pepperdine University, a student presented a video on Dostoyevsky's *Notes from the Underground*. This would not have been a worthy submission as the work of a film major. It did not have the technical success that would be rightly expected. But the video was extremely interesting to those students who had read Dostoyevsky. Similarly, three years earlier a student (now in a PhD program in English literature) wrote a poem about great books. This is also *scholarship* that is valued because it demonstrates the emotional connection that secures knowledge.

Jackson's sense of the poles of existence and essence echoes Ralph Waldo Emerson. Thought and action participate in what Emerson calls "that great principle of Undulation," or polarity, by which apparently opposite qualities actually depend upon one another and call one another into being.[1]

This suggests the Reality/reality that Knowledge is One, both poles required. Knowledge may often be associated with Essence, but it has to be realized in existence. Both are part of what is termed here *generative scholarship*. Intellectual life requires learning established Knowledge and creating new understanding. They function mutually with biofeedback, back and forth in an ecology of research and scholarship passed along generation to generation.

One of a teacher's former students, Karl, forwarded an e-mail from one of his former students, Kris. The forwarded message includes Karl's response to Kris. Karl wrote, "My mentor always said you're never prepared for the amount of failure you'll experience as a teacher." That teacher often makes that remark, but he is not its author. One of his earlier students, Julie, made that pronouncement in a class for student teachers.

The beauty of the example here is its fit with the book's understanding of educational legacy and the ecology of schools. A student taught the teacher who taught a later student who taught his own student. That's how it always works, just not usually so obviously. Such interaction is how the biofeedback model of research and scholarship tends to work at its best—and it is generative.

The term *ecology* has often been used to describe any complete system that relies upon the relation of its parts. For this book, the term *ecology* suggests all the necessary and interdependent roles that form the entire world of research and scholarship K–PhD. The term also suggests the need for protection. A common connotation of *ecology* is that the health of all the individual parts is necessary for a fully healthy system. This study identifies a gamut of considerations about research and scholarship. The thesis is that understanding and appreciating this diversity can improve policy and practice.

The terms *scholar* and *researcher* are both important to this work. They are not interchangeable. Separately, however, and used as terms in their original and broadest sense, they represent critical realities for an educator. A scholar studied in school with a master (or at least someone with more knowledge than the student). A scholar who conducts research looks for answers to questions, primarily by looking back at prior knowledge and personal experience. Thus the denotation of scholar is one who studied with a master. The denotation of research is to look back.

For many, perhaps most, the connotations of the terms scholarship and research imply stuffy, boring, pedantic. Alas.

When done well, being the scholar who works under a masterful teacher is challenging, vigorous, and enlightening. When pursuing one's questions, conducting meaningful research, the thrill of the hunt and finding even tentative answers to questions, and realizing new questions, causes one to feel like Miss Marple tracking down a murderer, Isaac Newton discovering gravity, Leif Erikson finding a new world, Langston Hughes writing a poem, Jonas Salk creating a cure for polio, Madam Currie realizing the significance of uranium.

Certainly, scholarship and research involves hard work, but the concern here is to focus on the excitement of curiosity. How is it that the public seems to talk only about assessment, standards, and state exams? The conversation must change.

Alexander Pope observed, "oft thought, but ne'er so well expressed." Many of the best ideas in education clarify issues students struggled with. For this author, a great debt is owed to Basil Bernstein and his ideas of *classification and frame*, Philip Jackson and the *hidden curriculum*, Elliot Eisner and the *enlightened eye*, John Dewey and *experience and education*, Decker Walker and his research that showed students do well on tests that measure what they were taught, Berlak and Berlak for the *dilemmas of teaching*, Jean Anyon for her insight into the influence of social class on the curriculum, David Tyack and the *one best system*. Optimistically, "When a lesson is needed the teacher appears."

Each of their seminal and formative ideas was a very different academic realization of research and scholarship. Bernstein did extensive field work, but his book was interpretive and theoretical. Eisner used aesthetic paradigms to think through complicated educational issues. Anyon conducted field research. Lee J. Cronbach argued that research was simply disciplined inquiry. These scholars used whatever means necessary to get at the problems that they were addressing. Based in research, their key contributions to scholarship were the quality of insight and the subsequent formulation of an idea that made it more possible for subsequent scholars to do their own work.

A healthy ecology of research and scholarship demands some very bright minds doing exceptional thinking. But arguably only a limited number of such ideas can shape a profession. The best thinkers need to provide ideas that influence the entire enterprise. But the predominance of educational work will need to be done by the rank-and-file teachers and professors (and their students). Together they must recognize and use the best ideas for those ideas to be sustained.

The scholars identified above all produced what Ernest Boyer has described as the scholarship of discovery. They also benefitted from the scholarships that have been identified by Boyer as integration, application, and teaching. All the teachers and students in the overall ecology need those best ideas. But statistically only a small percentage will have opportunity to produce the most influential ideas. A sound ecology exists when the best ideas are able to surface to the top. Meanwhile the entire profession and student body gets about the important business of teaching and learning, scholarship and research of their own.

This is not a passive business. The presumption here is that the best ideas are most likely to surface when all students and teachers, K–PhD, recognize that they are engaged in scholarship and research. The best ideas will only become obvious when teachers and students seize them because they are helpful to their own searches for answers to complex problems. All students and teachers are intimately involved in scholarship and research.

In a *real* sense this book is about the extended *school family*. This book offers evidence, observation, tales, lists, recommendations. The study concentrates on the myriad of academic approaches for studying lives and the world. As seems true of most family sagas the participants quarrel, fight, argue, harangue, dis, snub, insult, pretend to ignore. Yet for all of that, and yet for all the study, research, scholarship, achievement, it is still true and it remains meaningful, that $K=1$. That is, whether contained in letters, symbols, numbers, Knowledge is One.

Consequently, all acts of scholarship at every level are inter-related and are generative. Curiosity breeds inquiry, yields knowledge, which hopefully leads to wisdom. All the teaching, learning, service, research, scholarship, colleagueship are part of a single ecology. The integrated academy deserves respect and full appreciation.

This study does not limit itself to a narrow understanding of research and scholarship. Knowledge demands special appreciation for all the many ways all students and teachers contribute to the whole. Students play a vital role in research and scholarship. Faculty and students are part of the same biofeedback system, the same ecology. All ongoing research and scholarship benefit from the checks and balances of teaching and learning.

The venerable Philip Jackson of the University of Chicago pointed out how educators have the simultaneous responsibility to grasp at the truth in all that they teach, while understanding that any such knowledge must be realized specifically in and by each student. This is a variation of the old question of whether a tree that falls in the forest makes a sound if no one was there to hear it. Is anything truly known if it cannot be passed along to someone else? The argument here is that the answer is "No."

Because of this, teachers and students alike are constantly and simultaneously trying to clarify Reality (in the general) and the real (in the particular). The ecology of school has its own biofeedback system. The particular informs the general and vice versa.

Accomplishments by a scholar result in biofeedback throughout the system. For example, Erik Erikson theorized about developmental stages. After approximately a generation of discussion, the school family decided that his *theory* was so accurate that it is often thought of now as being merely descriptive.

Benjamin Bloom researched stages of cognitive thinking. He created the taxonomy that moves upward from Knowledge to Comprehension to Application to Analysis to Synthesis to Evaluation. A generation of study later that next generation determined that Synthesis was Creativity and was actually at a higher level of cognition than Evaluation.

Lawrence Kohlberg researched stages of moral reasoning. The ink had hardly dried on the page when his Harvard colleague, Carol Gilligan, argued that his Stage Three thinkers (more often women), were actually at a higher level of moral thinking than those at Stage Four (more often men). That was not the end of the sometimes heated family discussion. Kohlberg took enough criticism about his Stages VI and VII that he abandoned them. He did so somewhat reluctantly and defensively, explaining that rarely did anyone test at a VI or VII anyway.

The point here is that each of these scholars worked at an institutional setting in the context of academia. Each of them undertook research that became extremely influential. Their scholarship was so widely regarded, the results were criticized and then modified. (That should be seen as a good thing, a healthy ecology.)

The downside to their respective successes is a familiar family problem. Their high level of success makes for invidious comparisons. What about the other family members, of different interests and talents, and teaching loads? Especially those who worked just as hard, but without such acclaim? Those who worked under entirely different expectations, workloads, and had different kinds of accomplishments?

Superficially, the faculty in higher education are in a star system. A faculty member who wins, for example, a Nobel Prize, garners print for the school in the national and local media. The kind of work that would earn a Nobel Prize deserves such acclaim.

But the great preponderance of the advancement in human understanding is accomplished by the rank-and-file teachers and their students and their supporting constituencies, which include publishers, administrators, accreditation agencies, grant sources, institutes, and the like.

K–PhD human curiosity and the impetus for raising and answering questions must be cultivated. Epistemological questions abound K–PhD. What constitutes valid knowledge? How do we know what we know? Decisions about what is most important in the curriculum are made at the federal, state, county, city, local levels. Eventually, as influenced by students, the teacher makes judicious choices about implementing those expectations. Theory and practice are interdependent.

A major assumption of this study is that to the extent all students and all teachers engage in what is associated with the terms *scholarship* and *research*, human understanding will increase in both the general and particular. Best ideas only diffuse throughout a system when they are critiqued for accuracy and relevancy, understood by others, and communicated appropriately. Without the skills of having learned from masters and having conducted one's own search for answers to questions, the greatest research effort would be like the tree falling in the forest with no one to hear.

Celebrate the stars' individual successes. But do not make it a prototype for others. Even the stars' overall success is largely dependent upon all teachers and students attending to their particular responsibilities to research and scholarship. The biofeedback of the entire schooling system clarifies, refines, adopts, adapts, propels the conversation forward.

There should always be a premium on the scholarship of discovery. The argument here is that the ecology of research and scholarship demands the attention of all students and teachers K–PhD. A university certainly profits by its recognized superstar publishing scholars. But the whole cannot function without all of its seemingly countless roles. Some scholars respond thoughtfully and insightfully to others' works, like they did in the cases of

Erikson, Bloom, Gilligan, and Kohlberg. Others translate those original works into books, articles, and textbooks that further disseminate those ideas.

Teachers explore ways for helping their particular students realize these ideas as accurately and meaningfully as possible. Students who grapple with these ideas have their own work to do. They can research these ideas in other writings, in discussions with their teachers and classmates, in thinking about their own life experiences, and in their own research. Their work may help clarify nuances about these ideas. All of this *best* occurs in a healthy system where each part supports the whole.

Academia is its own biofeedback system. The faculty and students constantly appraise and reappraise making ideas real. And sometimes all of this biofeedback leads to a reappraisal of the understanding of Reality itself. The work, or the understanding of the work, becomes modified. Individuals may stand out, but it is all very much a team effort, a community undertaking.

NOTE

1. See more at http://www.enotes.com/topics/american-scholar/reference#sthash.UzKizqAq.dpuf.

Chapter Ten

Establishing the Rationale and Grading Policies for Student Scholarship and Research

> One can remain alive . . . if one is unafraid of change, insatiable in intellectual curiosity, interested in big things and happy in small ways.
> —Edith Wharton

Not such difficult questions.

How can a teacher justify time spent on any activity not directly related to the subject matter being taught? Time on task studies find that the more time spent on task yields higher test scores. However, time on task studies focus only on the results of instruction, and teaching-learning involves much more than that.

With homage to Abraham Maslow's Need Hierarchy, a teacher must have classroom discipline and keep students involved. Some teachers have used the game *Jeopardy* to review class content, especially prior to an exam. That game format is an extremely inefficient way to cover course content, but in certain situations can keep the students involved and moving forward.

Each year in school, teachers socialize students to specific educational identities. Teachers are not merely conveyors of specific knowledge, although that is critically important at every level of schooling. Teachers model ways of behavior that students may emulate, or at least consider in making personal choices. Teachers may be on task, even when not specifically on their subject matter. The socialization to the skills of modern living are probably much more important long-term lessons for most students than learning about the ostensible subject matter.

How can teachers justify, for example, the time spent on a service-learning project as part of the curriculum? The best way to learn a subject is probably to teach it. Students tutoring other students in the subject matter would have great merit for both service and mastering the subject.

However, a much wider sense of service has potential to make a significant educational contribution to most any class, even if the service is only tangential to the class subject.

Philip Jackson (1968, 33) coined the term *the hidden curriculum*. The term refers to the implicit lessons taught to students about social skills. K–PhD teachers teach what Alex Inkeles described as the skills for modern living. In K–PhD, even at the doctoral level, the teacher is not likely to have even one student who will finish the degree that the teacher has earned in order to teach that class. Consequently, no student likely wants to learn everything that that teacher would have them learn.

Yet students at least intuitively know that they are learning something that may help them later. Like time management. Schools can be so caught up in subject matter assessment that they lose sight of their overall mandate to turn out future citizens. Students may pass a math class where they learn to divide and multiply fractions, but be unable as adults to increase or decrease a recipe accurately. But the further they go in school, changes, presumably positive ones, occur.

When done well, the intentional curriculum can be covered in less time than the time allotted. Students also have responsibilities for the class outside of class time to cover course content. Teachers can make time for a full education, including one that emphasizes a true sense of scholarship and research. It is not only justified for students to spend time seemingly off task, but such is absolutely necessary for a full education. Learning skills for living are the long-term goal of any curriculum.

That is the reality. Quality subject matter remains especially important, but not at the expense of everything else. Every text has a context and students need to learn how that knowledge fits with other knowledge. Maturing as learners and humans, they are socialized into the skills for modern living.

Thus, for example, meaningfully constructed service-learning opportunities socialize students to the expectation that knowledge leads to lives of service. Quite possibly the service engagement will lead students to pursue their own questions that stem from that service. Such activity is consistent with the professional expectations of most college faculty: teaching, scholarship, service, and colleagueship. The scholarship of service responsibly finds the best place for service for any given school.

The long-term effects of scholarship and research are much more extensive than what comes from the scholarship of discovery. The scholarship of teaching, service, the student, curriculum development, and colleagueship all contribute to human development and understanding.

THE LONG-TERM EFFECTS OF EDUCATION

Ernerst Pascarella (2005) has studied the ways a college education affects students. Again, since most students will not go on to major in the subject the teacher is teaching, more than knowledge of the subject matter is vitally important.

Certainly in learning and cognition, the students' learning starts with greater knowledge of the subject matter. But regardless of the subject students:

- become more critical, reflective, sophisticated.
- improve their reading and writing skills.
- use their acquired skills from the social sciences, math, science, and art for solving problems.
- develop advanced critical-thinking skills and a critical-thinking disposition.
- utilize reflexive judgment-thinking.
- have a more mature epistemological sophistication.

Much more is involved than just the accretion of academic knowledge and skills. In terms of psychological change, students:

- experience a decline in authoritarianism.
- have a more intellectual orientation.
- have a greater sense of psychological well-being.
- are generally more autonomous.
- are more independent of family influences.
- have a more developed identity and social self-concept.
- overall have more self-esteem and a sense of independence and control over their lives.

Certainly, some of these overall results are due to the cocurriculum, but the preponderance of hours students spend in school are in the classroom or on classroom assigned activity. The teacher's efforts and effects in constructing a meaningful curriculum go far beyond only teaching of the subject matter.

Similarly, attitudes and values change. Students:

- have an increased interest in the visual and performing arts.
- place a higher value on the intrinsic rewards of education.

- move to the liberal end of the sociopolitical continuum.
- become less doctrinaire in their religious values.
- are more committed to gender equality.
- are more tolerant of other political, social, and religious views.
- have more knowledge of social and political issues.
- are more likely to vote and be politically active.

In terms of moral development, they (students) tend to move from conventional to principled reasoning.

Another way of thinking about why to expand what is included in the curriculum is that each course simultaneously teaches subject content and social skills. The subject content should be important, but the emerging attitudes, moral development, and social skills have the greater lifetime effect.

Similarly, Harvard professor and sociologist Alex Inkeles (1968, 50–68) identified skills for modern living. Along with the intentional curriculum, each teacher might hope to teach students:

1. respect for other cultural, ethnic, and social groups, relative freedom from racism, sexism, and other prejudices.
2. to be informed as a consumer in terms of establishing the value of a product or service received.
3. to have minds tolerant of diversity, not insisting everyone share his/her opinion.
4. the ability to insure protection of one's interests, to avoid being cheated or defrauded and preserving one's security, esteem, and career.
5. to have minds that have some compounds of flexibility to consider new ideas and adapt with the times as necessary.
6. acceptance, understanding, and appreciation of others.
7. information about and ability to identify when and where to go for what, whether for business, consumer, or personal wants and needs.
8. skill in interacting with adults on an equitable basis whether initiating contact, discussing mutual interests, or resolving issues.
9. defense to control and channel acceptably the impulses to extreme dependence on parents and authorities.
10. skills in negotiation to protect both self-interests and others' interests.

Inkeles's list of these skills is longer yet, but the point worth repeating is that each teacher has a particular responsibility to the subject being taught. But the teacher also has to ensure that the implementation of the curriculum tends to meet all the long-term needs of all the students. Helping each student be a scholar and researcher, and at least occasionally utilizing methods borrowed from other fields, increases long-term understanding throughout the ecological system.

GRADING CONSIDERATIONS

Even at the college level, how do teachers grade student work outside their primary subject-matter preparation? One way would be to have such work graded on a criterion-referenced basis. Each person gets an agreed-upon number of points if the criterion are met; and have to do it over if not. Certainly some students will outperform others on such activities; it becomes a good opportunity for the class to discuss the meaningfulness of intrinsic rewards.

At the K–12 level, symbols can be used to give students feedback on seemingly nongraded work. A scale of +, √+, √,√-, and 0 is much like an *A*, *B*, *C*, *D*, and *F*, but does not have the same emotional weight for students. There is more than one way to show excellence. If a student has a string of +s, that indicates something to consider when it comes to the final grade. And surely everything doesn't have to be graded?

Students might also be asked to critique something, say an unusual piece of art. Students could decide on their own whether they think it good or bad. And after that discussion ends, the teacher could give them a critique written by an expert. The teacher should emphasize that the students do NOT have to agree with the expert. But they should question, did the expert see something that they did not? Or what did they see that had more or less value to the critic than to the members of the class? Excellent books exist about teaching methods. The emphasis here is on recognizing the relationship of academic skills and social skills to enhancing scholarship and research among students from the earliest of ages.

This study includes proposed New Carnegie Units (appendix) as a way of promoting fairness in how different forms of scholarship and research can be quantitatively weighted. The qualitative evaluation of scholarship and research also has great importance. While more difficult to measure than the quantity of work, two general principles are more easily defined. The arts and humanities rightly emphasize the importance of the relationship between form and function.

John Dewey observed that the purpose of criticism is the reeducation of perception. Each form of scholarship and research deserves to be considered on the basis of its own assumptions. One would not use the criteria used to judge a Woody Allen film to judge a Steven Spielberg film; one would not use the criteria used to judge a Warhol painting to judge a Picasso. A primary question for all scholarship and research is how the form meets function.

However, the form and function question tends to emphasize technique and not the quality of the content. A painting can be done well or poorly, a literary analysis well or poorly, an experiment in the lab well or poorly. The hours one puts in on typical academic assignments set one standard for comparing the time and effort put into different forms of scholarship and research. The temptation might be to judge the quality of those efforts by the traditional letter grades of A, B, C, D, and F.

Such a choice would be ill advised. One of the primary reasons for letter grades is a matter of sorting and selecting. As a student negotiates a curriculum, the student discovers what s/he is best at. Eventually some of the best and brightest end up in a PhD program where general excellence is expected. For example, the grade of "C" might jeopardize one's graduate standing. Presumably most of those who became professors earned mostly grades of "A" in the final years of their terminal degree. *Grading* good professional work with the grade of "B" seems ill advised if only for teacher morale.

Nonetheless, by the time one is finally finished with school, one has a sense of what is "A" work, excellent work, and one knows that all one's efforts do not meet such lofty standards. High school Honors English teacher Alice Coleman maintained her high standards by giving students an "A" in the class if the student could earn an "A" about one time out of four. Review committees presumably want to set high standards without overly discouraging the need to take on scholarship and research that does not always meet the highest standard.

The cumulative influence of school is far more profound than only the acquisition of subject matter knowledge. The time spent on covering the subject matter, and all the time spent with students and the assignments teachers assign to students, is doing the heavy lifting of an education. In terms of overall learning, the time in the classroom is implicitly always on task. The thought here is that all the time in class and all of the assignments start with teaching the subject matter and its assumptions, but that equal thought needs go into all the ways that make for well-educated students and lifetime learning.

Another way of thinking about why to expand what is included in the curriculum is that each course simultaneously teaches important subject matter and critical social skills.

Chapter Eleven

No Good Deed Goes Unpunished; Virtue Is Its Own Reward

Warnings and Encouragement

Experimenting with forms of research outside those most common to one's academic discipline has risks. No good deed goes unpunished. This is especially true at the high school and collegiate levels. Will virtue be its own reward?

WARNINGS

Really?

The scholarly article was accepted by the philosophy journal. Then the editor discovered that the professor was from a field other than philosophy. The article was cancelled.

A physical education professor was selected to spend a year to represent America at the Olympics. A very important, but time-consuming job. The professor did not get a promotion because of lack of scholarly articles during that time. The university would have preferred that s/he stay home and work on an article to be read by seven people?

A college working toward a cultural diversity not historically represented on campus had a professor produce a multicultural theatre event. S/he spent more time on this production than might be spent on a book. All aspects of what was selected for the show were based in careful study of historical texts. And the event was determined to be only *service* but not *scholarship*.

The senior faculty member experimented with two forms of scholarship used by Erasmus: the Enchiridion and Satire. Such efforts of arts-based research were deemed unseemly, to be avoided, and that the professor needed to specialize.

The professor, at the behest of the university, was hired to create a more meaningful role for the scholarship of service. And was warned by many that such efforts would likely never lead to tenure.

The professor led a nationally recognized debate team, coordinating all the research that has to go into preparation for the issues assigned at tournaments, but had a paucity of articles. The extensive research working with students on debate topics was not considered research or scholarship.

The professor wrote a historical novel hoping to get students more interested in a less-than-popular time period and then was mostly criticized for not producing conventional research.

The professor had had a number of public gallery showings of his/her paintings, but was advised to write it up in an article.

The professor had a number of successful books, but couldn't teach her/his way out of a wet paper bag. Recognized as a *distinguished scholar*.

At a pharmaceutical school, only those who didn't do the exhaustive hours of the clinical work had the time to write the kind of articles for tenure.

The professor was a social pariah because of the lack of research, but handled the class load well. In fact, the person was ailing. Dismissed just before dying of cancer.

The professor was a nationally recognized scholar on *women's issues*. She was not granted tenure because she had ostensibly failed to advance her discipline's field.

Three out of four professors who earned Teacher of the Year honors were not granted tenure.

Really?

The beauty of scholarship and research by teachers, professors, and students is that whether individual or collaborative, it tends to be self-actualizing. As Abraham Maslow found in his needs hierarchy, self-actualization is the highest human need.

Thus, conducting one's own scholarship and research at every grade level K–PhD meets a human need. Such effort transcends the needs for external rewards. That is fortunate. Appreciation is rarely forthcoming. One continues with extraordinary scholarship and research because virtue (and self-actualization) is its own reward.

Nonetheless, being prepared is being forewarned. Noteworthy educational undertakings draw flack. The urban school district principal consistently bragged in public about his school's school within a school, while trying each year to shut it down (until he finally succeeded under the pretense of a district-wide budget crunch). Control was more important than the work done by that program.

Rafe Esquith, a nationally recognized school teacher, writes of having, for example, to meet his cocurricular program outside with his students one year despite, or because, of his acclaimed success.

Some days such heroes feel like Peter Finch's Howard Beale from the movie *Network*. "I'm mad as hell, and I'm not going to take this anymore." But on the good days the answer to the question of was it worth it is, "Of course." Such are the perplexities and contradictions of life.

Ernest Boyer (1990) observes the conflict among scholars and their approaches to scholarship and argues that diversity is necessary. Varying modes of inquiry and standards for that inquiry must necessarily have at least a modicum of tolerance and respect.

Yet within the academy, where a rank, tenure, and promotion system prevails, how are scholars of such different orientations to be compared? Also, to what extent can a scholar of one tradition be allowed, even encouraged, to experiment with a form and method of scholarship associated with a different discipline?

The answer lies in the nature of schooling. Educators must multitask. Inherently, academicians are expected to stay abreast of developments in their field and pursue disciplined lines of inquiry of their own. Besides continuing personal academic development, a scholar is expected to teach students. Did the students learn and grow?

Schools are also institutions created to serve the community, both locally and beyond. Thus especially at the collegiate level, professors are evaluated on their scholarship, teaching, service, and colleagueship. Inevitably, some make greater contributions in one area than others. A consistent standard of scholarship is excellence. Conventionally, scholars most similar to the one being evaluated come to some judgment about the relative merits of the individual candidate for advancement in rank or promotion. How do they evaluate the utility of the scholarship, the teaching, the service, the colleagueship?

A historian visits gravesites of heroes of his own religious movement. Those visits become stories for sermons that this scholar preaches at his church. While this work may have limited value to a wider, more scholarly audience, this research inspires this scholar. Rarely do scholars evidence such purity of intellectual curiosity. His most immediate community profits from his research as well.

Another scholar has both a gift of synthesis and an all too rare rapport with students. He writes textbooks that students actually want to read. More than a few become captured by the immediacy of the subject and go on to become majors, and virtually all of the students become more knowledgeable about the subject. The text has been adopted by numerous other universities. Whereas it is thought that perhaps only seven people read any given scholarly article in its entirety, thousands reading one scholar's textbook has great utility, not only for the increased knowledge of the readers, but for the perceived prestige of the university as well. Such scholarship communicates the results of original scholarship to students.

Yet another scholar has developed a curriculum in service learning that has been adopted into the university's curriculum and each year more and more classes now include a component of service learning. Alumni report that they have been engaged in community service because of the influence of this aspect of their undergraduate curriculum. Occasionally a service opportunity leads to a career opportunity.

No one ever knows where a teacher's individual influence ends. Teacher to student, scholar to scholar.

Who better than the scholars to research what deserves attention in school? Inevitably, a full education requires a great diversity of responses by students and teachers.

When an institution fails to remember the necessary diversity of the faculty, the following is a case in point about what can happen.

A lot of professors' career arcs are set in the early years. If one professor teaches in an Honors program, someone else is not. The patient, mild mannered professor was popular with students who struggled. And he wasn't a hard grader. Only half a class can be in the top half of the class. Only half of a faculty can be in the top half of lowest average grade point averages for the school.

In the early days of his career at a relatively young college, he was one of the first to frequently write books. He found a niche in writing on popular issues from an academic perspective. Over the years, however, the college grew in academic stature. Instead of teaching eight courses a year, the new faculty taught as few as five. As the faculty grew in prestige, the criteria for academic writing changed. University presses became preferred.

As the younger faculty assumed major committee roles, it was not only that this older professor was left somewhat behind, he became derided for the softness of his scholarship. But for him, that ship had already sailed. He was entrenched in the kind of work that he did well. He would not suddenly be sending extensively footnoted articles to journals with very low acceptance rates. But for a long time, he kept writing the kind of books that he was good at, and spending his usual inordinate amount of time talking with students on campus. He continued to be subject to snide criticism about his books and relatively easy grading.

Then one year he just said, "No." No more books for his readership that in numbers far outstripped the readership of the scholarly journals. No more easy grades. No unnecessary time on campus. He flunked perhaps half of his classes. Athletic teams were suddenly decimated by the lack of eligible student-athletes who had needed that one "B" to remain eligible.

Langston Hughes asked what happens to a dream deferred? What about a dream that loses its place of respectability?

Boyer's understanding of necessary diversity is necessary to meet the very diverse needs of an educational institution. Not every professor had the opportunity for cutting-edge scholarship of discovery. But each and every professor's work is informed by research and scholarship. The reward system needs some level of appreciation for all the work that needs to be done, or it won't get done. This appreciation also needs to recognize the different arcs of careers started at different points of the respective university's history.

One definition of scholarship is simply the work done by scholars. Whatever work they do is inevitably informed in some way by their ongoing work as scholars.

In evaluation, time spent is one of the considerations. But not the only one. If Albert Einstein could get a day's work in the patent office done in an hour, congratulations to the supervisor who allowed him to spend the rest of the work day on mind experiments in physics.

Stephen Crane's *Red Badge of Courage*, which was written in two weeks, is a worthy book, and so is James Joyce's *Finnegan's Wake*, which took him thirty-five years. However, if any given professor has approved duties that take up more than the half the work week devoted to teaching, concessions in expected number of publications demand to be made. Also, *academic freedom* entails the right at different points in a career for the professor to devote time to areas of curiosity regardless of whether the results end in publication. Intellectual curiosity deserves latitude.

Boyer recognized it as necessary diversity. This author cooperates and contends from the first day of school to the last, and then at graduation sits and marvels at how few of the graduates were his own students, and how necessary each and every one of his colleagues were not only for the graduates, but for him having such a context for such a meaningful career.

IRONY

The larger-than-life actor Charlton Heston observed that he had thought his time on the set of *Ben Hur* was the most exciting time of his life. Curiously, he had kept a diary during the film shooting of that epic, Oscar-winning picture. In running across his old diary, he found to his great surprise that what he had written was a litany of complaints. The weather was too hot, the food terrible, stomach ailments, lots of quarrels, and he was bitten by one of the camels.

Extending oneself to pursue one's own questions as a teacher, professor, student, scholar, researcher has that contradiction. Exhausting while invigorating. Charles Dickens captured it with his observation in *A Tale of Two*

Cities, "It was the best of times, it was the worst of times, it was the age of wisdom, it was the age of foolishness, it was the epoch of belief, it was the epoch of incredulity."

INTRINSIC REWARDS

Out-of-the-ordinary efforts have risks. A professor determined to host a *Pnyx*. So, what is a *Pnyx*? The original *Pnyx* was a public meeting place in Athens. Citizens of the democracy met there to make proposals and proclamations. This *Pnyx* was an opportunity for students to make proposals and proclamations, and also to showcase the range of their academic interests and work. It was an academic talent show.

The *Pnyx* had the creative dimension of creative scholarship. But its primary purposes included eliciting original, course-related, and publicly presented work by students, and to promote a sense of a learning community among the participants. It was time consuming, had serious heuristic intent, was informed by scholarship, was above and beyond the usual teaching expectations, and combined service with scholarship.

How are such efforts not only to be evaluated, but given the protection of a recognized and legitimate use of a professor's time? The hope is for the protected academic freedom to experiment, to take risks, to get out of one's comfort level, to animate one's research and scholarship. Such should be possible throughout a career, not just under the protection of already being a full professor.

Preparing students for advanced study or mentoring them for major awards are especially important acts of scholarship. Every aspect of our ecology of education has import. Each individual makes choices about their roles and responsibilities. Some choices will result in greater salaries. Some choices will result in greater prestige. But every role is important. And every role will be better performed by the educator who consistently exhibits the best most appropriate forms of scholarship and research toward increasing human understanding.

This study started in frustration but ends with optimism, admiration, and praise. Teachers K–PhD do not always fully appreciate each other. They are all doing important work and do it best when they have had their own good teachers. When they continue to research their past and the work of others for the benefit of students, they transform the world.

APPRECIATING THE STARS

Professional athletes are extremely competitive, and tend to have an exaggerated sense of their own talent and importance. Yet the players on a Los

Angeles Lakers Championship team got together and bought the highest paid player on the team a Rolls Royce for his birthday.

Kareem Abdul-Jabbar had made playoff money possible for each player. That level of team success also raised each player's likely salary for the next year. Apparently there was no professional envy, just appreciation for the superstar who made it all possible.

On my professor's salary I am not quite yet willing to chip in for a Rolls Royce for any of our research stars, but I appreciate the value they bring to the entire educational enterprise. Even Kareem Abdul-Jabbar could not have won a championship by himself. A team effort was still required. The other players had necessary roles.

Apparently John Dewey was a very boring teacher. But he wrote important, influential, highly regarded books. Honor him and overpay him.

Theodore Roethke was an English professor who wrote great poetry. Recognize the poetry as arts-based research, make him full professor, overpay him.

Spike Lee wants to teach film. Give him an honorary doctorate and hire him.

Such exceptional people provide great benefit to the whole. Appreciate it.

Instead of standardizing expectations for any particular teacher on a faculty, set high standards across all areas of scholarship, and when one has a very valuable faculty member, appreciate what is, instead of holding up some sort of standardized expectation that cannot possibly fit all. Students, alumni, constituents, colleagues will appreciate the wisdom.

Too often school boards, or boards of Regents, or school administrators mistake the work of the handful of superstars as a model for all teachers. Such is a tremendous disservice to all.

Schools rely upon its faculty to have the flexibility to cover all of the many needs of scholarship, teaching, service, collegiality, committee work, advising, assessment and evaluation, management and administration, extension, community, continuing education, mentoring.

EVALUATION

Having wise evaluators is incredibly more important than specific methods of assessment. No quantitative measurement will suggest the difference between *Annie Hall* and *Lawrence of Arabia*. Rubrics can help as a reality check, but never substitute for the holistic evaluation of the most perceptive critic. Because all areas of scholarship have their own special dictates, finding the most suitable form of assessment remains a challenge.

Educators can use numbers as reality checks, but never hide behind them. What would have happened to Bob Dylan if he had auditioned for the television show *American Idol*? Most professors deserve some trust. No one arrived at a professorial position without a vast amount of commitment and hard work. Most professors have a level of intelligence that would suggest that they have at least as good an idea as anyone else in terms of how they can best use their limited time. Those who really are not suited for the work usually become readily apparent, and are sorted out of jobs even before any formal proceedings.

Would it not make a lot of sense to assess how many legitimate and important hours/units a teacher has already put in on behalf of all the university's interests, before dictating the numbers of publications? The argument here is that evaluation is best done when the individual professor is assessed in how well they did his/her particular job, than by invidious comparisons to those with radically different subjects, workloads, and even history of service to the specific school.

In terms of utilitarianism and the standard of the greatest good for the greatest number, great personal value that has minimal cost to others retains great value. In evaluating scholarship and research, the audience might include the public, specialists in the field, others in higher education, the K–12 schools and their constituencies, a school, a classroom, an individual student, self.

Certainly, scholarly articles in elite journals garner and deserve recognition and praise. But a full accounting of a teacher's work needs to also consider whether the work done has kept the teacher vital, and whether individual students have been mentored so well as to carry that scholar's influence far beyond what a published article might have.

BON MOTS

Yogi Berra said that "when you come to a fork in the road, take it." As an educator, try a method of scholarship and research that challenges your comfort level. Remembering the frustration and exhilaration might well spark a whole new line of inquiry.

Even though the results are much more tenuous and tentative, action research will get the practitioner closer to the mark.

No good deed goes unpunished; virtue is its own reward.

Be well advised that going above and beyond is likely to create as much resentment and even hostility as recognition and approval.

As usual, this is the best of times and the worst of times in education.

We need evaluation, not just assessment.

If the purpose of scholarship is knowledge, then the purpose of knowledge is wisdom.

Examples of knowledge are always best understood in the context of a whole. Thus reading, and reading widely, remain critically important to understanding any significance of any acts of scholarship.

All efforts of research/scholarship are efforts of "trying to make it real, compared to what" (jazz musician Les McCann).

No academic inquiry was worth it if it was at the expense of intellectual curiosity.

Students and teachers should not focus only on what they are best at.

Are the results of scholarship more pertinent to understanding the facts of life, or in finding meaning in that same life?

Conclusion

> The important thing is not to stop questioning. Curiosity has its own reason for existing. One cannot help but be in awe when he contemplates the mysteries of eternity, of life, of the marvelous structure of reality. It is enough if one tries merely to comprehend a little of this mystery every day. Never lose a holy curiosity.
>
> —Albert Einstein

DEVELOPING STUDENTS

How does the teacher develop students as scholars, as researchers? Develop students' curiosity, their inquisitiveness. Their talent at asking good questions. Their reading skills. Their ability to use resources to find answers and their ability to distinguish credible knowledge and sources.

Because our definition of scholar is of one who studied with a master, teachers might do very well to let students in on some of their choices in constructing a curriculum. Why one book might be more suitable than another. Why an assignment is in response to a tendency for students to believe what they find on the Internet. Why a study requires the use of primary and secondary sources. Why an artistic opportunity involves them researching, looking back, and mining their imagination, or personal experiences, of a subject before expressing a personal outcome.

At least since Socrates, students have benefited by experiencing how teachers think out loud. If students start the process of seeking answers to questions in kindergarten and continue it for twenty-two years of schooling, K–PhD, they might find they like it and get pretty good at it.

Even all teachers K–PhD would do well to engage in forms of scholarship and research outside of their specialization. The broader meaning of both research and scholarship contextualizes all of the efforts to learn in an ecology that increases human understanding.

No matter what the field of study, students will have more depth of understanding if they have entertained both scientific and artistic perspectives on the field. If John Dewey is correct, their knowledge will be made complete by having both intellectual and emotional understanding. Besides, the teacher needs to keep every student involved because the long-term effects of an education rely upon keeping the student in school.

SET HIGH STANDARDS; DON'T STANDARDIZE

Substandard professors are often screened out of their positions by administrators and peer pressure before they get very far in the rank, tenure, and promotion system. Once professors have established sufficient worth to keep their jobs, the task becomes to set high standards, *not to standardize*. Also, while providing great service, an entire faculty cannot be in the top half of overall performance.

How does one value the stars and superstars without making for invidious comparisons for the rank-and-file professors without whom there would be no students earning college degrees? Curiosity remains fragile. Students and teachers need encouragement.

Public schools all eventually did away with merit pay because such a program was found to cause more ill will among teachers than happiness among the few who received such extra pay. But colleges and universities are less democratic, and certainly any school would want to recognize, by extreme example, a professor who had won a Nobel Prize. More important than any system are wise decision makers. Realistically, the perceived bottom half of a student body or faculty may need the greater encouragement. Especially at the college level, the teachers are probably carrying more than their fair share in teaching and advising loads.

What rating scale might be used that recognizes that virtually all professors are making a contribution, but that some do an even better job? Certainly for those professors on the fast track, the school would look for "consistent excellence"; for those on track, "evidence of excellence"; for the critically important rank and file, "valued" contribution to the ecology of scholarship and research. And for those times when for whatever reason a professor has had a slump, a recommendation for "renewal and re-review."

Whatever the form of scholarship, besides questions of reliability, validity, robustness, and rigor, at least a precursory look at other variables would seem in order. Were the results of the research pertinent to the cognitive, psychomotor, and/or affective domains? What is the relationship of the study to how students engage the subject studied? Are the results pertinent to how people learn subject matter, or how they inspired in meaningful, life-changing ways? How do the results contribute to the understanding of the general, longest-lasting results of a lifetime?

Dewey's work has been very influential in the author's career in education. The author has had opportunity to speak with a handful of Dewey's former students. Each of those students reported that in the classroom Dewey was extremely boring.

Would the ecology of education be healthier if Dewey had, for example, spent more time with action research, studying his own students and developing his own curriculum, improving his teaching? Or was the profession best served by Dewey's prolific writing? Were they exclusive of each other? Who is to say?

However, the hope here is to challenge the thought to do only what one is best at. Not to neglect one's strengths, but that if kindergartners through the research stars were to go beyond their comfort levels with scholarship and research, the whole system would benefit.

Set high standards for overall success. Otherwise students and teachers may confine and constrict themselves to the detriment of the whole.

While tempted to title the conclusion with the immortal words of miscreant Rodney King, "Can't we all just get along?", the emphasis more appropriately belongs on some sort of dynamic tension between cooperation and conflict. While something was lost when psychology abandoned philosophy for a separate academic home, when teaching abandoned curriculum (at AERA) to become a separate division, when anthropology separated into separate departments (one of science, one of humanities) at a major university, otherwise unresolved conflicts have often created new opportunities.

The two cultures C. P. Snow recognized as art and science have the capacity to provide checks and balances between the relative standings of truth and meaning. Together the two perspectives have the capacity to create depth of vision. While dissertations invariably profit by the advice to "delimit, delimit, delimit," the plea here is that healthy conflict among approaches to scholarship must not delimit and discourage further possibilities.

Whatever the local dominant paradigm, a healthy regard for the *loyal opposition* should be of paramount importance. Ernest Boyer opened up the possibilities with his recognition of the importance of the scholarships of discovery, integration, application, and teaching. The subsequent discussion has added a greater concern for the art done by professors, art-based research, scholarship of service, community/extension/continuing education, assessment and evaluation; curriculum development, academically informed management and administration, and while not a form of scholarship per se, the importance of professional collaboration.

Conclusion
ART AND SCIENCE; K=1

A greater balance between artistic and scientific paradigms probably exists in schools than is commonly imagined. But the scientific assumptions continue to dominate the discourse about what is presumably important in education. From the behavioral-objectives onslaught of the 1960s, individual educational plans, and assessment, all emphasize identifying a problem, gathering data, and reaching a conclusion.

The renowned educational psychologist Lee J. Cronbach and Suppes (1969), surprisingly for a noted social scientist, emphasized that research for tomorrow's schools consisted only of *disciplined inquiry*. Empirical studies governed by strict scientific principles of procedure are not the only way to understand and improve school.

Yet even the term *disciplined* assumes an unnecessarily narrow definition of empirical. As Elliott Eisner has explained, art is also empirical in that it is based in experience. *Disciplined* is not necessarily the way artists tend to go about their work.

To backtrack slightly, knowledge is in no way limited only to what is taught and learned in school. But what is known, and taught, and learned in school is shaped by how school masters (and again a scholar is one who has studied with a master) teach students to research (look back). Together, teachers and students go back over accumulated school knowledge and personal experience to pursue improved understanding. Hopefully, the quest is driven by vibrant curiosity.

Creative artist scholars do not necessarily set about their work in what is ordinarily thought of as systematic and disciplined ways. Artists tend to be more likely to take in all that they can. They consider prior knowledge, feelings, experience, impressions, musings, imaginations. Then in fairly ineffable ways, they work out all that they have taken in as they use the medium they are working with to see something new.

Education has historically made more of a dichotomy between art and science than actually exists. Especially in the elementary school years, teachers are likely to give students much more latitude to do artistic work instead of term papers. Such latitude for students need not end in elementary school. An assumption of this book is that by enhancing scholarship and research among all students and all teachers at all levels, using art and science, together they will increase human understanding throughout the ecology of education.

A critically important implication of the relation of scientific and artistic inquiry, *creative scholarship* fulfills all that is meant and intended by research. Certainly scientists have admirably set a high bar of expectation, especially for what Boyer terms the *scholarship of discovery*. However, what

Ernst Cassirer describes as the necessary relationship of science and art for bifocal depth of vision, Eisner describes as necessary for full cognition.

What Boyer recognizes as necessary diversity suggests that creative artistry is not only necessary as a complement to the traditional, academic emphasis on scholarship of discovery, but necessary for the inquirer to have a fulfilled sense of all that is entailed by both *research* and by any academic discipline.

Every academic subject demands some dynamic relationship between the science and art of its subject. Scientists, and scientists as teachers, often experience the artistic imagination vital to a successful experiment or lab. Artists and artists as teachers attend to the math of the canvas height and width, the chemical properties of varying types of paint.

Surely any academic career profits by attention to the overall influences of the schooling experience, whether through art or science. Einstein's experiments were most often *mind experiments* that required a level of imagination more often associated with art. The Pointillists reacted to the science of perception as their updated impressionism. Art and science share the pursuit of human understanding.

Diversity within teaching is important: might this not equally apply to some amount of diversity within the individual scholar's career? The very word *research* means "to look again." Eisner (1991) points out that both artists' and scientists' work are empirical in that both are based in experience. Within a career, a painting professor might very well profit by writing a peer-reviewed article, and the social scientist by painting a cognitive map, if only for her/his students to see the benefits of finding multiple ways to organize knowledge.

Undertaking methodologies that are not central to one's academic discipline offer the advantage of depth perception and full(er) cognition. The downside is what might be perceived as the inefficiency of a nonmastered methodology. The upside includes that different students may be coaxed into interest in the subject matter in any number of creative ways.

The upside is also that the individual teacher will have contributed not only to his/her own depth of perception and full cognition, but also to his/her full humanity. The teacher and the classroom can only be better for this.

The most rigorous scientific study often started with imagination and creativity before the undertaking of the research. Research on the brain suggests that each scholar would exhibit fuller cognition by adding forms of scholarship that s/he hasn't been using in his/her overall repertoire. Scientists should not only give respect to art, but engage in it, and vice versa.

So why such conflict about art versus science, qualitative versus quantitative research, science-based versus arts-based scholarship? Blame the Greeks and their tendency toward bimodal thought. Blame C. P. Snow and that his two cultures of science and art tended to become a self-fulfilling prophecy of divisiveness.

At least through the eighteenth century, academia evidenced no such strict dichotomy between art and science. As Machiavelli observes, people can hardly be faulted for taking things that they want, so do not entirely blame the logical positivists for the dominance of the scientific paradigms. But whether truth is to be emphasized with the scientists, or meaning with the artists, science is vacuous without meaning and art is shallow without truth. Because K=1. The entire academy creates and preserves knowledge.

Again, "K" represents the letters and stands for knowledge. The = sign stands for symbols, whether as musical notes, punctuation marks, icons, images, signifiers, and so on. The number 1 stands for mathematical ways of knowing. Knowledge Equals One whether it is discovered in science or art, and however it ends up being represented by letters, symbols, and numbers. This understanding of knowledge presupposes that all forms of scholarship fit into one ecology. Each part has a vital and sustaining role for the whole.

Further, the premise K=1 works regardless of whether it entails that Plato's forms do exist, or whether Jean Paul Sartre's existential accumulation of subjective knowledge prevails. Whether truth exists as an objective, independent form, or is the subjective accumulation of knowledge, Knowledge is One. All forms of scholarship generate the material that may lead to wisdom. K=1. It is all a part of a single ecology. All parts need to be healthy.

EDUCATIONAL JARGON

Sometimes there is utility to educational jargon.

The upside of developing a professional language is that it can improve communication among people in the same area of interest. Effective and efficient. The downside is that it becomes jargon difficult to be understood by anyone outside of the immediate field.

Certainly since the advent of language, words have been used to identify insiders and outsiders.

Time Magazine once wrote that a renowned minister and Civil Rights activist could talk about theologian Paul Tillich to a fourth-grader. Clarity is certainly preferred over obfuscation. However, a handful of well-chosen terms can be extremely helpful in developing an intellectual rationale for an educational idea.

Well-selected and defined terms can help others understand the depth of thought behind a proposed, purposeful action. They can help give confidence to the decision makers that the proposer just might know what s/he's talking about.

Teachers periodically seek permission to take students on field trips. Understandably, administrators need to justify any expense and time involved with a trip. Inevitably, the first request from administration will be for intended objectives and how the results will be assessed.

The sight of schoolchildren filling out pieces of paper in museums is painful. Museums are for exploration. Museums at their best create marvel and celebrate curiosity. What better way to kill a field trip than to make it tedious with a bunch of directions and assignments?

Eisner coined the term *expressive objectives*, which he later amended to *expressive outcomes*. No administrator really prefers for kids to be bored to death. But they have responsibilities to a school superintendent and school board to justify what they allow. Any application that cites an expert like Eisner, has prima facie serious heuristic intent. Activities like a field trip can best be evaluated after the fact. Students can individually express their individual learning outcomes. With such a rationale the application is likely to be approved by the decision makers.

Because the intellectual defense is sound, it is professionally responsible. It also reassures the bean counters. Students are spared the ignominy of carrying pencil and paper around a public museum. Curiosity and exploration, critical to their development as scholars and researchers, is honored.

ABOUT TEACHERS

Having already used the metaphor of biofeedback, antibodies are vital to human biology. Experienced teachers have experienced the unceasing calls to yet another new innovation. They are understandably wary of any new and imposed program. They know that there are no cure-alls, no panaceas. New fads come and go constantly. A faculty president once observed that his school would be much better off if the administrative travel budget was redlined. What he meant by that was that if they could keep administrators from traveling to conferences, they could end the yearly administrative expectation of yet again adopting some new idea.

Most teachers already have more ideas about what they might do than they can achieve. They need more time, not imposed new requirements. A chance to pursue some of their own ideas just might invigorate them.

James Herndon wanted to title his book, *Notes from a School Teacher*, *Teachers are the Franchise*. Teachers often feel beleaguered by what gets written about them in the media. Actually the public think teachers are only behind ministers and doctors in the perception of who contributes the most to the public good. Parents with children in school rate their children's schools as highly as or higher than at any time in the past. (It is helpful when one reads all of the research.) But teachers tend to feel unappreciated. The daily discourse about assessment standards and test scores is such a limited way of talking about the school experience. It is no wonder that teachers have to monitor their discouragement levels.

There is no teacher-proof curriculum. Even if it has come to teachers having to prepare students to meet set standards, teachers need and deserve the flexibility to find the best ways to work with their own students. (Schools are not made up of average kids. By definition, half are above average and half below. Whatever the generalizations, every kid is different in important ways and the teachers need the time and opportunity to spend part of their work obligations sussing that out.)

Teachers and professors need and deserve some freedom to salvage their own curiosity, to pursue their own questions. They earned some latitude by having put in the school work necessary to get where they are. Even if they pursue a question without finding an answer, it is often the pursuit that matters most and keeps them growing and vital.

Stunting the student and teacher initiative necessary for scholarship and research is not good policy. Teachers need the latitude to say, "I don't know," and to pursue questions, and sometimes to fail.

Teachers are busy enough with the have-tos of course preparation, teaching, grading, meetings, and so forth. At least in the foreseeable future, most of their extra effort will have to come at personal expense—where the intrinsic rewards must prevail. Professors presumably have more time to conduct research, although that amount of time varies greatly from institution to institution. But they, too, need the latitude to increase human understanding, and reach all of their students, by utilizing methods and approaches borrowed from other disciplines. Rank, Tenure, and Promotion systems need to be wiser about all that counts for scholarship. The appendix makes a case for a New Carnegie Unit that would provide a method for recognizing how time available in job descriptions influences what can reasonably be expected.

Fortunately, the skills of scholarship and research generalize. Every student K–PhD needs the opportunity to look back and say with appreciation, "I studied with _____."

Perhaps not all students are able to do that. But most probably are. The popular students and popular teachers have more obvious visibility. However, most often the teachers thought to be unpopular have their own, if smaller, following. Like attracts like. Different kinds of students find affinity with different kinds of teachers.

While teaching their respective grade levels and academic subject(s), consciously or unconsciously, teachers socialize their students. Professors are ordinarily evaluated in four areas: teaching-learning, scholarship, service, and colleagueship. Those four areas matter K–PhD. Assessment tends to focus only on the teaching-learning. Even at universities that regard teaching as the predominant responsibility of professors, scholarship, service, and colleagueship cannot be ignored. They are skills developed over years. They cannot suddenly be mastered after being hired as a professor. Furthermore, teaching-learning, scholarship and research, service, and colleagueship pertain to all lives.

Starting at home, advanced in school from kindergarten on, students need opportunity, experience, and teaching to develop all four capacities. *All* students need to develop in each of those areas. Future air-conditioning repairpersons, auto mechanics, bankers, teachers all need the skills associated with teaching-learning, scholarship, service, collegiality.

Recently, the author spent considerable time trying to fix the air conditioner in his recently purchased home. The author is strikingly inept at anything remotely mechanical. He called an air-conditioning repairman. The repairman failed. Fortunately, the author has research skills.

To make a very long story short, it turns out that this was a high-end air conditioner. The manufacturer no longer existed. It had been bought out by another company. Even that company sent the wrong part the first time. But by then the author knew the what and the where.

He would have preferred that the repairman had had such research skills. Students, no matter what their futures, need to develop research skills.

The auto mechanic could handle the basics. He was dependable and affordable. He would refer the customer elsewhere if it was a car problem he could not handle. In public, he was quiet and unpresupposing. He called no attention to himself. He was easily overlooked.

What was hardly known by others was that he was quick to respond to others' distress. He would give food, offer a ride, give some cash, lend a car, visit the sick. Without any fanfare. True modesty. Invaluable service.

Professors need not be surprised by the sudden service expectations of their jobs. The orientation to service should be inculcated from kindergarten on, for all students whatever their future careers.

Aristotle opined that we would not choose to live without friends. Isocrates identified one of the spirits of Greek Culture as *agron*, the spirit of competitiveness. This competiveness, however, was not about winning or losing. It was about improving individual performance.

Kindergartners can be extremely competitive. Schools foster competition to motivate students academically and athletically. Competition can be a very good thing when healthy. However, sometimes it seems like teachers should have spent more time in the sandbox than the library.

Schools have most of the same unresolved conflicts that society has. The author had opportunity to drop in on an English Parliament committee meeting. A funding proposal was contested by representatives of the rival political parties. The issue was real. The behavior of the two opponents was not only civil, it was respectful and even cordial. America needs to reclaim that aspect of its English legacy—appreciation of the loyal opposition. Colleagueship matters.

As scholars teaching young scholars, teachers must attend not only to teaching-learning, but scholarship, service, and colleagueship as well. How to be successful across all four areas? Einstein said that "success comes from curiosity, concentration, perseverance, and self-criticism."

Enhance scholarship and research K–PhD. For all students. Emphasize teachers as mentors, not only as instructors. Make time K–PhD for teaching-learning and scholarship and service and colleagueship. Do not neglect art. Value and use art and science in every subject. Help students ask their own questions. Help them look to past knowledge, experience, and all available resources and methodologies for finding answers and asking increasingly better questions.

The mission for all students and teachers as scholars and researchers: increase understanding; advance the quality of human life.

Extra:

Writing a book ordinarily involves writing chapters and thus involves creating meaningful classification schemes. Curiously, the individual incident that kept cropping up for the author was an incident that had a profound influence on his entire career in education.

Los Angeles's Occidental College sent a professor on an admissions trip to San Diego. A professor. Not a young admissions counselor or administrator from the Admissions Office, but a professor.

Certainly, the author can and will identify this as an example of service. That a professor was looking for students was a powerful statement about scholarship and research. Since the author prefers the definition of scholarship as what a scholar does, and that the trip was at the college's behest, the time he spent should count as more than just service, minimally the scholarship of service.

But that does not seem to be the important point. The historical definition of scholar is to have studied with a master. While the movie *The Karate Kid* was not set in a school setting, Mr. Miyagi reached out to a young man and became his teacher. The master connected with the student.

Nel Noddings (2007) has written about the three Rs of teaching: receptivity, reciprocity, and relationship. Ideally, the teacher will be receptive to each and every student. It is up to the student to reciprocate. Without that meaningful relationship and connection, meaningful teaching-learning is unlikely to occur.

Whether on admissions trips, an information day on campus, or how one meets one's students, establishing the relationship of teacher and student is vital to sustaining scholarship and research across all levels of education and across the generations.

Appendix A: The New Carnegie Unit

> Expectations for the amount of scholarship a faculty member contributes in any domain should account for time spent in teaching, advising, and service contributions. For example, a faculty member teaching four courses a semester and advising more than fifty undergraduates should not be evaluated for tenure based primarily on research contributions.
> Establish a committee on faculty workload to assess whether expectations for faculty contributions to scholarship are realistic, considering the balance of faculty responsibilities.
>
> —KerryAnn O'Meara (2005, 296)

There is a major problem for most college professors, at least those who are not at the top tier research institutions. The rank-and-file college professors teach perhaps twelve hours a week, and prepare for those classes another twelve, and keep office hours at least six hours a week, and serve on at least one committee. That leaves only a few hours in the work week for the increasingly expected research and professional service.

If college professors were truly meeting their professional obligations to students, a significant percentage of those remaining ten hours in the forty-hour work week would necessarily have to be spent on what Ernest Boyer identified as the *scholarship of teaching*, and most of that time would need to be spent on *research* and *scholarship* that pertains only to the respective professor's classroom.

The case here is not against the incredibly important *scholarship of discovery*. The case here is that in the names of justice and learning, professors have a professional obligation to *research* optimal ways of teaching and evaluating each and every class.

Lectures have utility, but with significant limitations. Commonly, only lower levels of knowledge and cognition can be covered in that format. For students to learn the skills associated with application, analysis, synthesis, and evaluation, other teaching-learning activities must be developed, and must be found suitable for that particular class of students, if maximum learning is to take place.

Because colleges provide such an important role for sorting and selecting students into yet further educational opportunities, those researchers who teach have a professional, and perhaps moral, responsibility to research *education* as it pertains to each respective discipline and how it is delivered to students.

Should a professor put in the requisite time to have a working knowledge of the research on teaching, learning, curriculum, the responsibility for still further scholarship remains. Full cognition in any field includes the creative and imaginative skills necessary for success in that field. One need not be an accomplished artist to explore the creative and imaginative possibilities of a field, and art becomes one of the best ways for realizing the emotional dimensions that accompany any field of study, especially the sciences.

Despite the great wisdom contained in Ernest Boyer's *Scholarship Reconsidered*, he neglected the implications and the importance of both the scholarship in education as it pertains to one's discipline, and the importance of the *creative artistry* that is implicit to all academic fields. Because of this neglect, Boyer tended to emphasize the public qualities of any work done in the scholarships of application, synthesis, and teaching. The impact of these forms of scholarship are as, or more, important for their influence on the classroom.

The professors' action research on teaching their subject, creating materials for their classes, and reaching their own students have great importance and worth. These aspects of scholarship need to make it more possible for the professor to be successful with the particular class. They need not be the kind of innovation that other teachers with other approaches adopt. A new practice need not work with other teachers, classes, and colleges to be worthwhile. The first and primary reason for these aspects of scholarship is to enhance the learning of one's own students.

Also, the great teachers utilize their classrooms as laboratories—where innovations do not always work. For the great teachers, their students are best inspired by the willingness of the teacher to stay fresh and to try new things on their behalf. The effect of caring and trying different strategies can be as important to students as any new model practice.

Professors tend to think about their teaching, scholarship, service throughout a given day, week, month, year. (Very often to the great annoyance of their significant others.) It would be impossible for them to account for billable hours. Given the extent of their credentials, most are modestly paid. It would be fair to limit their job expectations to a forty-hour work week. Most professors the author knows spend far more than that amount of time. But is it fair? is it right? to demand more than forty salaried hours?

Because for many, or most, being a professor is an avocation. Seemingly all the professors the author knows spend more than forty hours a week, and more than thirty-six weeks on their *jobs*. However, from a labor point of view, the level of *expectation* for professors to do research given their other job demands seems excessive, unjust, and counterproductive if teaching is an important part of that job. The professor could profit by a better way of accounting for what kind and amount of research and scholarship can be expected and accomplished. The professor's assigned work load has to be a factor in any such evaluation.

A NEW CARNEGIE UNIT FOR SCHOLARSHIP: A METHOD FOR ESTABLISHING COMMENSURATE VALUE AMONG THE OVERWHELMING VARIETY IN TYPES OF SCHOLARSHIP

In the most hopeful of all possible academic worlds, all forms of scholarship will have recognized value, and presumably most professionals will choose to do what they find most valuable, both personally and for the whole.

Typologies of research/scholarship have identified areas that include: discovery; integration; application; teaching; creative artistry; service; judgment/evaluation/assessment; management and administration; curriculum development. Forms for such scholarship have been argued to include: aesthetic and stylistic artifacts; performances; designs; paintings; sculptures; photos, shows; distribution of products, materials or programs; reviews; news reports; copyrights; patents; peer presentations; juries; publications; presentations; exhibits; developing new courses; revising courses; writing textbooks; creating innovative materials; instructional software; instructional manuals; peer-reviewed journals; presentations at professional meetings; external grants; reports on practice; certain forms of consulting; writing novels, plays, poems, film scripts, essays, satire, parody, editorials, handbooks, reviews; preparing a new course; designing a new course; assessment of a curriculum, program or school; the evaluation of a curriculum, program, or school, or school system; a prepared speech related to professional knowledge; presenting at a professional conference whether on a panel, poster board, group presentation, personal presentation; an accreditation report; an unpublished paper, monograph, or white paper; a published paper, monograph, or white paper; an unpublished book manuscript; a published book manuscript; a college textbook; a K–12 textbook; nonnaïve art (painting, film, dance, sculpture, play, novel, etc.); a professional consultation; writing a grant; creation of a new minor or interdepartmental program; creation of a new major; creation of a significant educational resource; developing a teaching-learning-related web site; seminar presentations; workshop presentations; extensive reading above and beyond the call to duty; journal editing; book editing; writing a chapter for a book; writing an encyclopedia entry; a book review; an unpublished book review; refereeing for a professional journal; mentoring a student for a PhD or national award; scholarship required for work with a national organization; scholarship required in the context of administrative duties; exhibition curatorship; library development; creating video and television programming; medical diagnosis; serving clients in psychotherapy; supervising student teachers; shaping public policy; creating an architectural design; working with public schools; working with private schools; creating pedagogical procedures that are planned, continuously examined, and related directly to the subject taught; well-prepared lectures (especially akin to those more commonly delivered in European universities); some popular writing; technical assistance; policy analysis.

What is still missing? All of the above when conducted by scholars undoubtedly include *scholarship* and have some significant amount of value. Furthermore, when one is involved in a particular worthwhile act of scholarship, there is less immediate time available for other forms of scholarship.

In a hopeful world of academia, scholars who emphasize work for their own school, especially those schools which are not seeking top-ten status, will not be penalized for scholarly work done primarily on behalf of their more immediate constituencies. Not all scholars need to identify more with their profession than their home school. So, how can we establish commensurate value among the overwhelming variety of types of scholarship?

THE NEW CARNEGIE UNIT FOR SCHOLARSHIP

Without getting into the technicalities of the historic Carnegie Unit, most secondary schools and schools of higher education have the general idea that a one-unit course usually meets an hour a week for fifteen to eighteen weeks. A secondary-school teacher works full time by teaching about five classes a day, five days a week. College students presumably do more independent work, and typical classes meet three hours a week for sixteen weeks as a three-unit course. A teacher is usually expected to spend about the same amount of time outside of class on grading papers, preparing lessons, and fulfilling assigned duties.

K–12 teachers spend about fifty hours a week during a school year, about half of that time in the classroom. College teachers more commonly spend about half that load on classroom teaching, but are expected to contribute more professional service, as well as produce significant academic scholarship. But how can oranges, apples, avocados, and professors doing different kinds of research, be compared? How does one compare a scientific research report with a historical novel, with a new art design, with a curricular innovation, with a textbook, with a seminal article? How do the scholarship expectations differ for a professor teaching three courses a year versus one teaching eight?

Introducing the *New Carnegie Unit*. This New Carnegie Unit approximates the original, historic, Carnegie Foundation method of counting course units as course hours. It has the same potential of being useful for measuring and comparing faculty loads. Note that neither system of units (the Old Carnegie Unit or the New Carnegie Unit) measures the quality of how those hours are spent.

Nonetheless, the students' required amount of time spent in a class over a semester, and the amount of time a professor must spend on teaching, scholarship, and service, is an important indicator of commitment. Especially with the difficult task of comparing professors across different fields, tallying the time they spend on meeting such expectations guarantees a certain amount of fairness in their respective evaluations.

Whatever the eventual academic specialty, virtually all educators have the feel, and most likely the experience, of having written a course paper; a term paper; a Master's thesis or Master's project; a dissertation; and quite possibly a book or major paper for a major journal.

A typical paper completed during a school course establishes the value of *one-half* New Carnegie Unit (eight hours of work). A term paper would ordinarily take about four times more time and effort for a weight of *two* (two hours a week for sixteen weeks, thirty-two hours). Sometimes a year-long course, or an extremely demanding final paper, would double weight at *four* (sixty-four hours). A Master's thesis ordinarily has about five chapters that have some kinship with term papers, but with the raised bar of expectation is weighted at ten times that of a term paper for a *twenty* (320 hours).

A dissertation is often longer and the expectations even more rigorous for a *thirty*. But the dissertation was only the scholar's first work, so the major article, or book, which often takes more than a year to complete, is weighted *thirty-five*.

There is an intended, nearly identical relationship of the Old Carnegie Units to the New Carnegie Units to quantify various academic activities.

Here are the two separate iterations in terms of how faculty loads and expectations might be determined on a semester system:

A Grid for Identifying New Carnegie Units

Grid for Identifying New Carnegie Units

	Hours	Number of Semesters	Total
Teaching			
Teaching Prep (one hour outside for each class hour)			
Office Hours			
Service and Scholarship			
			40 + one summer month

40 hours a week for 2 semesters = 80 New Carnegie Units
    One summer month = 2.5 New Carnegie Units
    Required units per year = 82.5 New Carnegie Units
    Thus at the author's university the grid of job expectation would look like this:

Grid of Job Expectation

	Hours	Number of Semesters	New Carnegie Units
Teaching	12	2	24
Teaching Prep (one hour outside for each class hour)	12	2	24
Office Hours	6	2	12
Available for Service and Scholarship			22.5

At the author's university professors are ostensibly evaluated on the basis of 50 percent teaching, 25 percent scholarship, and 25 percent service. If professors were only working a forty-hour week, merely 60 percent of the time available would be taken up by teaching. If office hours were counted as service, there would only be 17.25 New Carnegie Units per year for scholarship. That would allow a major article or book once every two years. And that presumes that the professor undertook none of the other forms of research valued in this book.

EXCHANGE WITH PROFESSOR JAMES THOMAS

I wrote Professor James Thomas because I admired his academic book on Harry Potter, but I also knew that he had received some criticism as an English professor for having written about a book that has had such success in the popular culture. I asked him how much time he had spent writing this book. Here is his response:

> I estimate that Repotting Harry Potter (357 pages) took me about 800 hours from proposal to completion. Based on approximately 450 hours per semester spent on a three-course, twelve-unit load from planning syllabus to grading final exams, the writing of the book I estimate to be the equivalent of 1.8 semesters of course work/teaching. I estimate my Rowling Revisited (199 pages) to have taken me about 600 hours, or the equivalent of 1.3 semesters' course work.

James's having kept track of the number of hours from book proposal to completion suggests that the author's estimate of a representative book might typically weigh in at 560 hours may be far too conservative as an estimated average.

If James had done no other scholarship, he met approximately four years of scholarship expectations with those two books. (Obviously professors willingly spend much more that forty hours a week on their avocations. Such time commitments are not resented when they are made out of internal demand rather than institutional expectation.)

James spent far more time on his job as a professor than could reasonably be expected. His success should be celebrated without it setting the bar for all other professors.

MEASURING/WEIGHING/ASSESSING DIFFERENT FORMS OF SCHOLARSHIP

Dear Members of the Teaching-Learning Committee:

My position is that to preserve our historical emphasis on quality teaching-learning, better ways of (a) preserving the necessary time for quality teaching against encroachments from other demands is of our concern; (b) our understanding of scholarship, particularly scholarship of teaching, demands full recognition.

Below you are asked to identify your own scholarship activities of the past year (since this in an inquiry, choose an approximately twelve-month period of your recent work) and then assign points to those activities based on the criteria that follow.

An issue of justice: whether your respective field tends to consider the following examples of scholarship, some field does, and the last twenty-five are from the Boyer model on scholarship. That is in no way to say that that makes each example of scholarship of equal weight. From my own point of view, I would think that the preparation of a lecture is covered in our 50 percent weight on teaching, but, nonetheless, I can imagine a lecture that goes so far beyond usual preparation as to warrant some extra consideration as scholarship. But, for example, my field is the "development and evaluation of educational programs," which is a central act of scholarship. I would think that others developing and evaluating curricula should receive a similar amount of scholarship credit for similar work.

I have changed the "points" for respective weight, primarily on the basis of my conversation with Xxxx, giving more weight to the dissertation and book particularly.

Quantity and quality of effort, quantity and quality of results are related, but not the same. We would need to be extremely careful that our attempt to find an approximation of weight does not become a fixed standard, merely an indicator that may help the conversation about scholarship and scholarship of teaching.

Scholarship	Title	Involvement Level
Preparation to teach a new course		
Design/creation of a new course		
Assessment/evaluation of a program		

Appendix A: The New Carnegie Unit

Scholarship	Title	Involvement Level
Assessment/evaluation of a meta-program		
Prepared speech related to professional knowledge		
Presentation at a professional conference		
Accreditation report		
Paper at a professional conference		
Unpublished paper or monograph or white paper		
Published paper or monograph or white paper		
Unpublished book manuscript		
Published book manuscript		
Published textbook—college		
Published textbook—K–12		
Non-"naïve" art (e.g., painting, film, dance, play, novel)		
Professional consultation		
Writing of a grant (successful)		
Writing of a grant (unsuccessful)		
Creation of a new minor or interdepartmental program		
Creation of a new major		
Creation of significant educational resources		
Web site development related to teaching and/or teaching areas		
Seminar presentations		
Conference presentations		
Extensive reading that did not lead to a paper or new course		
Edit journal		
Edit book		
Write chapter for a book		
Write for encyclopedia		
Book review for journal (published)		
Unpublished book review for an editor of a publishing company		
Peer review for professional journal		
Mentor a student for PhD or national award		

Appendix A: The New Carnegie Unit

Scholarship	Title	Involvement Level
Scholarship required for work with national organization		
Presentation/workshop to Seaver or Pepperdine		
Scholarship required in administrative capacities		
Exhibition curatorship		
Panel		
Preparing quality computer software		
Creating video and television programming		
Participating in curricular innovation		
Medical diagnosis		
Serving clients in psychotherapy		
Shaping public policy		
Creating an architectural design		
Working with public schools		
Pedagogical procedures that are "planned, continuously examined, and related directly to the subject taught"		
Well-prepared lectures		
Writing and other preparation for classroom presentations		
Opinion editorials		
Popular writing		
Consultation		
Technical assistance		
Policy analysis		
Program evaluation		
Musical recitals and performances		
Juried exhibitions of art work		
Dance productions		
Service on national committees		
Chapters in invited symposia		
Delivered addresses		
Revise a course		
Preparation of new teaching materials		
Scholarship of service		
Disciplined study of one's students		

Scholarship	Title	Involvement Level
Extension/continuing/community education		

F=Course paper=1/2
E=Term paper=2
D=Two term papers (i.e., the effort of a term paper but possibly the effort of two semesters)=4
C=Master's thesis=20
B=Dissertation=30
A=Manuscript/book/original scholarly paper=35

1. By reassigned time, sabbatical, reduced course load, how many courses less than six per year did you teach?
2. Is your métier classes under eighteen? In the vicinity of thirty-five? Large classes (50–250)?
3. How many different courses did you teach during the time period being assessed?

The lesser the teaching load, presumably the greater the expectation for service and scholarship.

Bibliography

Anderson, Gary, and Herr, Kathryn (1994). *Studying Your Own School*. Thousand Oaks: Corwin.
Anderson, Lorin, and Krathwohl, David (2001). *A Taxonomy for Learning, Teaching, and Assessing: A Revision of Bloom's Taxonomy of Educational Objectives*. New York: Longman.
Anyon, Jean (1980). Social Class and the Hidden Curriculum of Work. *Journal of Education* 162 (1): 67_92.
Apple, Michael (1977). What Do Schools Teach? In R. H. Weller, ed., *Humanistic Education*, 27–47. Berkeley, CA: McCutchan.
Barone, Tom, and Eisner, Elliot (2012). *Arts-Based Research*. Los Angeles: Sage.
Berlak, Ann, and Berlak, Harold (1981). *Dilemmas of Schooling*. New York: Methuen
Bernstein, Basil (1975). *Class, Codes, and Control*. New York: Schocker.
Bloom, Benjamin (1956). *Taxonomy of Educational Objectives*. New York: Longman.
Boyer, Ernest L. (1990). *Scholarship Reconsidered*. San Francisco: The Carnegie Foundation.
———. (1996). The Scholarship of Engagement. *Journal of Public Service and Outreach* 1 (1): 11–21.
———. (2015). *Scholarship Reconsidered: Expanded Edition*. San Francisco: Jossey-Bass.
Buber, Martin (1958). In Gregor Smith, trans. *I and Thou*. New York: 1958.
Clark, Don (2015a). Bloom's Taxonomy: The Affective Domain.http://www.nwlink.com/~donclark/hrd/Bloom/affective_domain.html.
———. (2015b). Bloom's Taxonomy: The Psychomotor Domain. http://www.nwlink.com/~donclark/hrd/Bloom/psychomotor_domain.html.
Cronbach, Lee J., and Suppes, Patrick (1969). *Research for Tomorrow's Schools*. London: The Macmillan Company.
Council of Arts Accrediting Association (2008). Creation, Performance, Research: Multiple Relationships and Possibilities. November.http://nast.arts-accredit.org/site/docs/CAAA%20Policy%20Brief/CAAA_Creation-Performance-Research_2009.pdf.
Eisner, Elliot (1979). *The Educational Imagination*. New York: Macmillan.
———. (1981). On the Difference Between Scientific and Artistic Approaches to Qualitative Research. *Educational Researcher* (April): 5–9.
———. (1991) *The Enlightened Eye*. New York: Macmillan.
———. (2000) Benjamin Bloom. *Prospects* 30 (3) September: UNESCO.
———. (2002) *The Arts and the Creations of Mind*. New Haven: Yale University Press.
Felder, Richard M. (2000). The Scholarship of Teaching. *Chemical Engineering Education* 34 (2): 144.
Freire, Paulo (1970). *Pedagogy of the Oppressed*. New York: Continuum.

Gage, N. L. (1979). *Educational Psychology*. Chicago: Rand McNally.
Glassick, Charles E. (1997). *Scholarship Assessed: Evaluation of the Professoriate*. San Francisco: Jossey-Bass.
Gose, Michael. (1999) *Creating the Winning Game Plan*. Thousand Oaks. CA: Corwin Press.
———. (2006). *Getting Reel*. Amherst, NY: Cambria Press.
Gurm, Balbir (2009). Is All Scholarship Equally Valued? Fusion of Horizons on the Definition and Status of Scholarship. *International Journal for the Scholarship of Teaching and Learning* 3 (2). Georgia Southern University. httm://www.georgiasouthern.edu/ijsotl.
iAnswers.http://www.ianswers.org/what-does-robustness-means-when-writing-a-research-paper.html p. 10.
Inkeles, Alex (1968) Social Structure and the Socialization of Competence. *Harvard Educational Review*. Reprint Series 1:50–68.
Jackson, Philip (1968) *Life in Classrooms*. New York: Holt, Rinehart and Winston.
———. (2012) *What is Education?* Chicago: University of Chicago Press.
Klein, Julie Thompson (2008). The Scholarship of Pedagogy (2) March.https://library.wayne.edu/blog/otl_newsletter/?p=464.
Kohlberg, Lawrence (1981). *The Philosophy of Moral Development*. New York: Harper and Row.
McLaughlin, Colleen (2004). *Practitioner Research and Enquiry: Researching Teacher, Researching Schools, Researching Networks*. Cambridge: University of Cambridge Press.
Mill, John Stuart (1988). In Edgar Knoebel. ed. *Classics of Western Thought*, 331. New York: Harcourt, Brace, Jovanovich.
Noddings, Nel (2007). *Critical Lessons: What Our Schools Should Teach*. New York: Cambridge University Press.
O'Meara, KerryAnn, and Rice, R. Eugene (2005). *Faculty Priorities Reconsidered*. San Francisco: Jossey-Bass.
Ortega Y Gassett, Jose (1980). *On Studying in the Series 10 Anthology*. Chicago: The Great Books Foundation.
Pascarella, Ernest (2005). *How College Affects Students*. San Francisco: Jossey-Bass.
Patsalides, Laurie (2015). *Putting Bloom's Taxonomy into Practice*.http://www.brighthubeducation.com/teaching-methods-tips/3648-using-the-new-blooms-taxonomy-kindergarten-classroom-example/.
Sagor, Richard (2000). Guiding School Improvement with Action Research.http://www.ascd.org/publications/books/100047/chapters/What-Is-Action-Research%C2%A2.aspx.
Selwyn, Douglas (2011). Encouraging Student Research. *Social Education* 75 (5) 277–80.
Snow, C.P. (1959). *The Two Cultures*. Cambridge: Cambridge University Press.
Steadman, Monty (2014). *Coaches' Guide to Cross Country and Track and Field: Training Cycles*. Monterey, CA: Coaches Choice.
Tyack, David (1974). *The One Best System*. Boston: Harvard University Press.
University of Chicago.http://press.uchicago.edu/ucp/books/book/chicago/W/bo12214939.html.
Walker, Decker, and Schaffarzick, Jon (1974). Comparing Curricula. *Review of Educational Research* (AERA) 44 (1): 83–111.
Weiser, Conrad (n.d.). The Value System of a University-Rethinking Scholarship.http://www.adec.edu/clemson/papers/weiser.html(accessed October 3, 2013).
Werber, Stephen (1992). On Defining Academic Scholarship. *Cleveland: Cleveland State Law Review* 40 (2): 215–16.
Wikipedia.http://en.wikipedia.org/wiki/Biofeedback</.

About the Author

Michael Gose, PhD, has taught and been an administrator at the elementary, secondary, and university levels. He has been a professor at Pepperdine University since 1980. He had the great good fortune of being a teaching assistant and research assistant to Professor Elliot Eisner at Stanford University in the 1970s.

www.ingramcontent.com/pod-product-compliance
Lightning Source LLC
Chambersburg PA
CBHW020742230426
43665CB00009B/523